Word to the Wise

"The Power of Perception"

By

Christopher Thomas Dwight Major Jones

Joneschris903@gmail.com

ISBN: 9780988410428

Printed in trey United States of America

Princeton TX

WORD TO THE WISE

AUTHORS NOTES

My main desire in writing anything and publishing it for the masses is to reach people. I feel that if I can reach one person and help that person understand and take my words to heart, I have done my job as an author. Most authors will say that writing will not make you rich unless you get lucky and come up with a best seller; I beg to differ. My first book has left me feeling like a millionaire because I have reached so many people and touched so many lives. I hope I can continue helping and inspiring others through my writing.

"Any fact facing us is not as important as our attitude toward it, for that determines our success or failure. The way you think about a fact may defeat you before you ever do anything about it. You are overcome by the fact because you think you are." — Norman Vincent Peale

DEDICATION

Inspiration has always been one of my main drives to continue to succeed and move forward in life. Without inspiration, I think we would all be in a social slump. My wife, Holly Jones, has been a true inspiration to me and I thank her every day for what she does for me and what we do for each other. Another huge inspiration was my father-in-law, Henry Lee Marshall, who passed away this year. He had a perception of life and real experience to match it. Reading a book to learn from someone else's experience is a good start, but first-hand experience is always king, and that requires you to trust and believe in yourself. We are only on this earth once. We get one shot and one shot alone.

I would also like to thank my mother-in-law, Geneva Coleman, for being a great inspiration. I want to thank my own mother, who has been there for me and taken care of me all of my life. I could fill an entire book with the names of each person who has touched me in some way. To my fans and all the people who have supported me, I can't thank you enough for being there for me and showing me that there is light at the end. You are the ones who inspire me to keep moving forward. Special thanks to my book mentor, Bella Zee, who is truly a great inspiration and has given me great guidance through the process of writing this book.

TABLE OF CONTENTS

~Chapter 1~

What does it mean to be successful?

After writing my first book, which focused on people with various disabilities, a lot of people have come up to me with questions. It is not a surprise that people want to know how I have found success, but what I find very interesting is the fact that many of these people do not have any disability.

This has led me to the realization that the desire to succeed and express the things that make an individual unique is a universal one that applies just as much to people with disabilities as it does to those without them. Moreover, people without disabilities are equally - if not more - capable of drawing inspiration from those who succeed despite having the odds stacked against them. I suspected my story would inspire people with disabilities, but I underestimated the response I would get from people without them. For many, the thinking goes like this: "If he managed to overcome everything that he did and find such astounding success, what is holding *me* back?"

Now that I see how my experiences can reach far beyond those in situations similar to mine and help people from all walks of life, I am inspired to write another book. This is not an instructional book or the typical "self-help" offering that will give you steps to follow in order to succeed. I don't believe that life can truly follow any one prescribed course.

Instead, I want to show others how ordinary people have found success, whether it's people I know personally, people who have shared their story with me after reading my book, or people I have helped. Everyone has a story to tell, and everyone's story is valid and meaningful. One person's path to personal success might not particularly move you, but the same tale could very well give another person the inspiration they need to achieve their dreams. Just like music and poetry are open to multiple interpretations, different people will draw different meanings from what I want to share with you in this book. At the same time, no one will walk away unaffected after reading this.

Success has a strong mental component

A lot of people think that success is about taking physical, observable actions. While this is certainly a part of it, a person's mindset plays a very big role in determining their outcomes in life. One thing that can hold people back from even a small degree of success is perception. This is something I will talk about in depth in the next chapter. However, it is important to realize how any seeds of doubt planted in your mind early in life can hold you back from becoming what you were meant to be.

We are very vulnerable in our formative years. Offhand comments made to us when we are younger can take on lifelike proportions as we get older and turn into debilitating thoughts that hold us back.

This applies not only to how others perceive you but, to a lesser degree, how you perceive others. Moreover, the way you treat others shapes their perception of you. If you were a bully in school, people will remember that as you get older and treat you accordingly.

I know from experience that having a legitimate issue in life does not mean that you cannot reach certain goals. But a lot of people are never able to break free of this mentality. It is easy to give up and say you can't continue or can't achieve something, especially when other people have told you this. Comments made by relatives, friends, teachers, and other people can have a big impact on your perception of yourself.

For example, let's say you always wanted to become a top basketball player. You practiced a lot and played with kids in your neighborhood. One day, one of the older kids criticized your ability to play. Maybe you really were playing badly, or maybe he was just having a bad day, or maybe he wanted to make himself look better, or he was trying to impress your girlfriend. No one knows why people say cruel things to others, but they certainly are not always true. Nonetheless, once it has been said, the damage has already been done, and even if you find out later that the person didn't mean what they said, it can be hard to undo the cascade of negative feelings that sprung from the hurtful comment. What starts as a small brick can eventually become the foundation of an entire house of negative thinking. It can turn you into a pessimistic person who thinks you have no hope so you don't even try.

I know this because I've heard it a lot of times. As an albino with a vision disability, you can imagine the kinds of negative blocks that have been thrown at me, even by people in positions of authority such as teachers. But rather than let them build up, what I've done is tear them down. A brick or two might be heavy when they are thrown at you, but when you let entire walls of negativity build up, think of how difficult it is to tear down a brick house.

Thankfully, there is a relatively simple way to tackle this problem: tear it down one brick at a time. You can't carry that weight for all of your life. Chip away at it, little by little, by changing your way of thinking and letting go of the past. People say cruel things, and often they are not true; they are coming from a place of negativity inside the person who is saying it that has nothing do with you and your abilities. Try to see those hurtful comments for what they really are: a reflection on the person making them rather than on you. Acknowledging the mental roadblocks that are holding you back and realizing you need to change your mindset are crucial first steps on the road to achievement. You have to free yourself from this defeatist attitude if you ever want to find success.

What is success?

A lot of people will say that they want to be successful. Have you ever asked them what that means? What makes a person successful? How is success measured? Some people have never really thought about it in depth. They don't know quite what it is but they know that they want it. Success can mean different things to different people, but it's universally agreed that success is something positive and something to strive for.

Merriam-Webster gives two definitions of success, and I think it is interesting to note the differences between the two. One is "the correct or desired result of an attempt." This is understandably broad and shows just how much grey area there is when talking about the notion of success. The other definition of success they offer is "the fact of getting or achieving wealth, respect or fame". This is a much more narrow definition of the term. While a great number of people do aspire to gain things like wealth, fame and respect, it is very telling that they feel the need to provide the other, more vague definition as well. After all, there are other things that can make a person successful besides wealth, respect or fame, and having any or all of those things does not always mean you have been successful.

A lot of people fall into the thinking that success is measured financially. How big is your bank account? What kind of car do you drive? These ideas are reinforced by our society. For example, look at music videos. They are often full of overt displays of wealth: Ferraris, mansions, jewelry, a harem of attractive admirers. For some people, these things are signs of success, but I believe that success is so much more than simply tangible items

You should also consider the fact that some people automatically receive these so-called success markers without putting forth any effort. For example, a person who inherits a big sum of money will have the fancy cars and nice houses, but can they really say they got all of it by being successful? No. They were just lucky; perhaps they were born into the right family. So money is not really a fair measure of success in every case, although it is something that some people strive for. A big bank account can indicate that a business is successful, for example. But it's not the be-all, end-all when it comes to personal success.

I believe that success is something that you have been through. It's an issue you have overcome, and now you want to help someone else overcome it. In my case, I feel successful because I do things in my life that give me the chance to help other people who face disabilities similar to mine. This not only helps them but it also helps me.

Inspiration and how it drives success

There are many things that can inspire us to become better people. When asked about their inspiration, there is a natural tendency for many people to think about individuals, a person who has inspired them. Indeed many people are inspired by another person. For example, my brother Rodrick has been a big source of inspiration for me. We were close and played a lot together when we were young, and we often spoke about our hopes and dreams for the future. I looked up to him and our interactions directly influenced my path in life.

. . .

This type of inspiration can be very powerful. When we look up to someone and want to be more like that person, it can spur us into taking action in order to achieve our objective. Of course, we have to choose our inspirations wisely!

It is important not to overlook the fact that inspiration does not always have to come from a single person. For some people, music can serve as an inspiration. Perhaps the words of a particular song really speak to you and make you want to do better and be better. That song can become your mantra. You can repeat the inspiring lines to yourself over and over to remind yourself that you are capable of succeeding. This can be very empowering for some people.

Other people might draw inspiration from a book. Perhaps you've read the biography of someone who has overcome obstacles or even a fictional tale about people who overcame adversity. Maybe you identified with one particular character in a book who inspired you to reach for the stars. Even an object can inspire a person.

Ultimately, it doesn't matter much where you find inspiration. The thing I want you to take away from this is the importance of having inspiration, regardless of its source. That inspiration is what will drive you toward success. Without it, you are just sitting at the start line with an empty tank. You might get there eventually if someone gives you a push, but inspiration will drive you from within and get you to the winner's circle a lot faster.

A few words on motivation

Let's go back to the music video example because I think it is something that can be really influential to impressionable young minds. The people in the video flaunting their wealth lead them to believe that they need the cars and the bling to be successful. While it's true that the people in the videos might very well be successful, they did not get there without having driven, inspiration, motivation, or a mentor. They are relaying their success by showing off what it can buy them, but it is important not to forget how these people got there. So when you see them and aspire to be like them, remember that the flashy lifestyle doesn't tell the whole story. You have abilities and talents but you have to believe in yourself enough to take action if you want to see success.

Although I have achieved a degree of success, you will not find me flaunting it. Instead, I choose to relay my success by helping other people to find their own success in life. I derive a great sense of satisfaction from using my experience to help other people overcome the obstacles that they are facing. I feel like success is contagious to an extent, and your success is my success. You are reading my book because you are looking for something that you think I have. I want to inspire you, I want to motivate you, and I want to help you get where you want to be.

~Chapter 2~

The Power of Perception

"You never get a second chance to make a first impression." Surely you've heard this quote before. Its exact origin is the subject of much debate, but no one disputes its validity".

In the last chapter, I touched upon how perceptions can influence us and even determine our success to some extent. In this chapter, I'd like to take a closer look at the idea of perceptions and their far-reaching effects.

How are perceptions formed?

College student. Recovering alcoholic. Computer geek. Church lady. What do you think of when you hear these terms? What emotions does each one inspire? Whether you want to admit it or not, hearing someone referred to as a member of one of these categories causes you to automatically reach some conclusions about them before you even meet them. The same is also true about some labels that can apply to me, such as blind, albino, or disabled. I know firsthand just how erroneous and harmful false perceptions can be. Even worse, they can be very, very pervasive.

Was there a particular food that you hated as a kid? Almost every kid despises at least one vegetable. Let's say in your case it was spinach, which is almost universally hated by children everywhere. So you're not sure why exactly, but you know you hate spinach because you always have. You've avoided it your whole life. Then one day, you are pressured into trying it again. Maybe you are meeting your girlfriend's parents for the first time and her mother cooked spinach. You decide you're going to force some down to avoid offending her. You tentatively put it on your fork and slowly raise it to your mouth, bracing yourself for the disgusting experience you are sure is about to come. You take a deep breath and put the fork in your mouth and you are pleasantly surprised. You discover that spinach is actually quite tasty! You end up asking for seconds. Then you ask yourself: why did I avoid spinach for all of my life?

The reason you've been missing out is because of the perceptions you formed when you were young. These perceptions are often formed so far in the past that you can no longer remember where they came from. Maybe your mom was too insistent that you eat your vegetables, so you declared your hatred for spinach as a way to assert your youthful independence. Maybe your aunt served you a batch of spinach that was slightly past its prime and you vowed never eat it to again. Maybe you ate it in the hospital cafeteria while you visited your dying grandfather and you didn't want any reminders of that traumatic experience. Perceptions are formed for a number of reasons, and some of them are quite silly in retrospect. Yet look at how strongly they persist. They become almost a habit, something that you do on autopilot without even thinking. This is when perceptions can become dangerous, because you don't even realize they are at play.

Maybe you still hate spinach, or perhaps you've always loved it, but I am sure there is at least one food you always thought you hated but then discovered that you actually loved when you tried it as an adult. This is an example of how strongly perceptions can shape our behavior. You shunned spinach or some other innocent food at every turn for years and refused to give it a second try until you were essentially forced to. Now you know how wrong you were. Is it possible this is also true about some other perceptions you hold?

Now that you can see just how perceptions rule over your decisions without your conscious mind even realizing it, think about how certain perceptions could be holding you back from reaching your goals or achieving your dreams. You can still have a fulfilling life if you somehow miss out on eating a particular vegetable, but the repercussions of other perceptions can be a lot more devastating.

There are two key components that go into forming a perception: information and experience. We do not learn things about people in a vacuum. Instead, we use new information about people almost as an afterthought, with the first impression being the overriding determiner of our opinion.

For example, you meet your sister's new boyfriend, who is a used car salesman. First you think of him as a used car salesman. Then you start talking to him and you find that he seems like a nice guy. He's pleasant and polite, and you enjoy talking to him. But he's still, first and foremost in your mind, a used car salesman and all that might go along with it based on your past experience or information you have heard from others. For example, you might have expected him to be dishonest because a used car salesman lied to you in the past.

Scientists call this schema-plus-correction. The schema is the prototype about the person ("widow", "attorney", "bookworm") and the correction is the information you learn from your first interaction with the person. These two things form the first impression, but unfortunately the schema tends to carry more weight in the process. So it's easy to see how bad experiences and bad information lead to inaccurate perceptions.

How can you improve your perceptions? First, don't be afraid of new experiences or repeating a past experience to see if something different happens. Second, seek out new information from sources you can trust. As simple as it sounds, it can actually be quite difficult to do this.

Psychologists have studied perceptions extensively, and they have reached three very important conclusions:

1. Perceptions are easily formed.
2. Perceptions are difficult to change.
3. Their influence persists for a long time.

Now, the good news is that people have a tendency to give each other the benefit of the doubt and view someone in a generally positive manner until the person does something to change that. On the other hand, humans also have a tendency to fixate on negative things. On top of that, people seek out information that supports their first impression. After all, who doesn't like to be right? This is a natural human tendency and one big reason first impressions and perceptions are difficult to change.

Think about it. If you think a new coworker seems like a nice, competent employee, you will probably overlook it if she slips up and chalk it up to first-day jitters. On the other hand, if you thought from the start that your new co-worker seemed like an idiot, the first time she snags a sale, you might tell yourself she just got lucky.

Perceptions are persistent

Why are perceptions so persistent? The answer is simple and yet it's so pervasive. We treat people in a way that often elicits the very behavior that conforms to our perception of them.

The highly regarded self-help author Wayne Dyer illustrates this phenomenon quite nicely with his famous saying, "When you change the way you look at things, the things you look at change."

I still remember an incident when I first started programming. I was friendly with nearly everyone I worked with in IT and I found that most people were helpful and supportive. So it really shocked me when one of my co-workers said to me one day, "I'm not sure how you're doing this." I asked him to explain, thinking that he was referring to a project we were working on, but it turned out he was thinking on a much grander scale. He said, "I'm not sure how you can be programming when you have a vision problem."

In one sense, it's actually a pretty fair question. It's even one that I've asked myself before. But it turned out that his question wasn't coming out of curiosity about how I managed the physical aspects of the job. He continued to tell me that I should not be able to do the things I do. I assured him that I was very experienced in my field and also educated, and he continued to ask how I managed to do all these things. I explained to him that I was extremely driven. I set my sights on my goal and I didn't stop until I achieved it. I worked hard and strived for what I have. Eventually I got the bottom of his line of questioning: He was jealous of me. He told me so explicitly.

Now I actually find myself changing the way I act when I'm around him. I tone down certain things and we speak to each other differently. All of this is a response to his poorly formed perception of me. Perceptions are powerful and they heavily influence our interactions with other people.

A lot of people don't know that I have a vision disability. Even though I sometimes hold a paper one inch away from my face, they somehow don't realize it. It is always interesting and thought-provoking to go in for a job interview. We are often told that interviewers make up their mind about a job candidate within the first few seconds of meeting him or her. Even if they don't make a hiring decision in that moment, they at least decide if they like the person or not. This ties in with how quickly first impressions are made and how difficult they are to change.

The interviewer won't ask me why my hair is the color it is or why my eyes move the way they do. They know on some level it will change their perception. A lot of times, there is something in the back of an interviewer's mind that tells them not to dislike someone because they are disabled. If someone shows up for the interview in a wheelchair, for example, the interviewer might think, "I can't hire this guy because he's in a wheelchair," but at the same time, he is often thinking, "I can't perceive this person this way. It isn't right on a moral level and it's also illegal." When I go into a job interview, the people conducting the interview don't even know that I have a vision disability. They don't ask if I have a disability, even if I indicate that I do in my application, which is something I find really interesting.

So at the end of this particular interview, I let them know that I do have a disability, and their entire attitude changed. It was a typically tough IT job interview, but this brought it to a whole new level. When I told the interviewer about my disability, he said, "I'm so sorry." And the interview became odd and uncomfortable after that. Once I said I was disabled, the interviewers let their perceptions color their view of me.

Although being on the receiving end of a faulty perception can be a negative experience, this isn't always the case. In fact, I once had a coworker who didn't know I was an African-American. He saw my white complexion and yellow hair and it just didn't occur to him that I could be black. He was filling out some Equal Opportunity Employment paperwork and noticed that it said we had one black employee. He thought it was a mistake because he didn't see any black people working in our office. We talked about it and he speculated that maybe the person who worked there before him could have been black. The entire time, it never occurred to him that the person could be me.

I admit that I let his guessing carry on for quite a bit because I wanted to see what his perceptions were about black people. He's a nice guy, and he never made a racial slur. So finally I told him that it was me. After three years of working together, he had no idea. He said, "Whoa, I didn't know that." I had actually thought he did know I was African American prior to that day. So he said, "Well, that solves the problem," and got back to the report.

His reaction was subtle but this information did indeed change his perception on some level. In this case, however, we still have a good working relationship. Other times, the outcome can be different, even to the point of losing friends.

We often make up our mind before giving a fair analysis

When I explain the concept of perception to people, I like to use the example of going to buy a car. Imagine that you are walking through the Mercedes lot when the salesman shows you the top-of-the-line model. "This is our luxury car," he says, as he shows off the leather seats, sunroof, seat warmers and extra horsepower. It's a very impressive ride. After that, you head over to the Infiniti dealership and are greeted with a luxury car that boasts similarly impressive specs.

Finally, you go to the Kia dealership. The Kia salesman says to you, "Let me show you our luxury model." It's a nice car, but the moment you see it, you start comparing it to the other cars you saw. Perhaps it is a luxury car compared to other Kia models, but it doesn't meet your perception of what a luxury car is that you formed when you saw the Mercedes. The Kia might be marketed as a luxury car because it is the best-appointed car in their line, but it doesn't hold a candle to the Mercedes. The perceptive mindset causes you to analyze the car before you actually even drive it. If you had driven it, you might have found that it was much more likeable than you expected it to be based on your first impression.

This is what happens with people as well. You analyze them based on past experience with someone similar and then compare them unfairly, and chances are, you don't even realize you are doing it. If only we could look at each car in isolation, if we only we could look at each person in isolation, we might be able to reach a more just conclusion.

How perceptions can cultivate fear and ruin lives

This brings me to a story a friend told me about a woman he worked with. All of the employees at their company had to take a mandatory test online before leaving work one day. It turned out that this woman had a reading disability. She was dyslexic and couldn't read the text.

She was terrified because no one at her company knew she was dyslexic, and she knew that finding out would change their perception of her. I know from firsthand experience that people with dyslexia are perceived differently, and this perception is not always a positive one. So she didn't ask for help out of fear that people would perceive her differently or not want to be her friend. She couldn't bring herself to ask for help because she would be forced to admit she had a reading disability. Ultimately, she decided to accept the punishment for not being able to complete the test at work and took the chance of getting written up or even fired so she could finish the test at home.

She said it was worth taking this chance, that the possibility of getting fired was better than having to admit the truth. She said that most people at her job perceive those with reading disabilities as having a mental problem, and she had even observed them making fun of such people. That is a case where a perception that might seem harmless has the potential to transform a person's life.

This goes back to how I tend to let other people figure out my disabilities rather than telling them about them outright. This dyslexic woman did the same thing. It's normal to want to befriend your coworkers. You'll be spending lots of time together and you'll need their help at times as well. And through interacting with them, she found out that some of her coworkers were inclined to make fun of people with disabilities.

This is something that has made me wonder, where do people get this idea of a reading disability being a mental problem? Do they get it from TV? Their relatives? Did their parents teach them that or set a bad example by making fun of people?

When I was young, I'll admit to making fun of people. But when my friends and I made jokes with each other, everyone knew it was in good jest, like the typical "Yo Mamma" type of jokes. We made fun of each other to elicit laughs, not to hurt feelings. We knew not to hit below the belt. We based our jokes on harmless things. No one ever made a joke about my disabilities.

No one ever said, "Chris, you're so blind, you can't see your way out of a will-lit house." We never made "wetting your pants" jokes with the kid who had a bladder control problem. We were raised not to make fun of a person's disability. Whether they are good or bad people at heart, my friends at least had the good sense not to be cruel.

Perceptions and labels

Even what is considered a disability is based to some degree on perceptions. Visual impairment is an obstacle, not a disability. Yet society has managed to make it a disability. The government has labeled it as a disability and I know that this has been helpful to people in terms of having protection and certain rights, but at the same time, the term can have defeatist connotations. We'll go into that more in the next chapter when we talk about labels, but I think anyone with any sort of disability can do themselves a world of good by thinking of it as an obstacle instead. After all, obstacles can be overcome. Reframing our perceptions can be as simple as changing our vocabulary.

Improving your self-perception

Now that we've established just how powerful perceptions can be, we can begin to find ways to use that power in our favor. How do you see yourself? What are your dreams? What is holding you back from achieving them?

Perhaps you want to be an Olympic runner but you think you're just not fast enough. Where did you get that idea? Who told you that? Is it true or is it just a poorly formed perception that is persisting?

. . .

I have a friend who wants to write a best-selling book but thinks she doesn't have the talent. While it's true that she hasn't struck gold yet, with that attitude, I want to tell her that she never will. I asked her, "Do you really and truly not possess an ounce of talent?" She admitted she's a better writer than a lot of people, but she still thinks she's not good enough. After some talking, we got to the root of the problem. The first agent she queried rejected her. This is pretty common in the writing world, but the rejection hurt. She felt like she wasn't good enough and that attitude has crushed her progress. It is only by breaking out of these harmful thought processes and improving our self-perception that we can unlock the key to achieving our dreams.

I can't tell you how many times I was told in my life that I couldn't do something. "You have a vision disability."

"You're an albino." People were negative toward me. Perhaps they thought they were being realistic and maybe even saving me from disappointment. It's not uncommon for people in my position to hear such comments. I think what makes me stand out and what helped me achieve so much is the fact that I didn't let those comments change my opinion of myself. The truth is, they were speaking not based on the truth but rather based on perceptions that were not properly or fairly formed. Realizing that they were just using flawed perceptions in making their comments enabled me to see past what they were saying. It was all based on faulty logic, an unfair assessment of me based on preconceived notions that had nothing to do with the reality of me and who I am.

It was my inner belief – my positive perception of myself – that enabled me to reach higher than those people ever thought I could. It is extremely difficult to put such thoughts aside, to ignore what people in seemingly higher positions than you – teachers, adults, successful people – think you are capable of. Take note, because this is what separates the winners from the losers: the steadfast belief in your ability to succeed. Even if you're not totally convinced deep down, the mere act of telling yourself you are bright and capable can reap enormous rewards and give you a big push down the path to success.

Now let's revisit that quote I mentioned earlier, "*When you change the way you look at things, the things you look at change.*" You can surely see how that applies to people as well. Now I want to ask: what about yourself? Can you change yourself by changing the way you see yourself? You bet!

~Chapter 3~

Overcoming Labels

I hope that your increased awareness of the power of perceptions from the previous chapter has changed your perspective at least somewhat. Now I want to talk about something that goes hand in hand with perceptions and is equally transformative: labels.

I think that anyone who has ever been hurt by having a label thrust upon them can benefit from trying to understand why people do this in the first place. When you think about it, the tendency for humans to label others is fairly reasonable. Our world is full of stimuli and it's useful to have a way to talk about certain groups collectively.

Let's take the example of skin color. Did you know that the color of people's skin covers a continuous range, with no two people having the exact same shade? You could line up a hundred or even a thousand people and not find one complete match. It is not practical to think up an infinite number of names to describe each person's skin color, so it is generally broken into two categories: black and white. This is a simplification of the process of categorizing people, and yet the social and economic repercussions of the labels of "black" and "white" on a person are staggering. What sounds like a very simple thing transforms lives and influences outcomes.

A self-fulfilling prophecy

The way labels shape perception has been the subject of many scientific experiments. In one such study, a young girl was described to half of the study participants as coming from an upper middle-class family and shown playing in a well-to-do neighborhood. The other half of the participants were told the same girl lived in low-income housing and her parents were blue-collar workers. All of them were then shown a video in which the girl was asked some academic questions and then asked to rate her academic level. Interestingly, the people who were told she came from a middle-class family rated her academic level as being higher than those who believed her family was low-income.

This is something that is seen time and time again, and further studies have yielded similar results. Perhaps the opinion of a group of study participants won't have much effect on this young girl's life, but imagine that the people in the study were actually her teachers. How would their expectations shape her academic success and, by extension, her job prospects and outcome in life? What do you think happens when a teacher is told a student is disabled? Even the most even-handed teacher can't help but be influenced by hearing this label. It's simply human nature.

People can't help but label others. It can even be traced to survival. Labeling certain spiders as poisonous can help people avoid getting ill or dying. If labels were simply descriptive and nothing more, they would be helpful. Unfortunately, labels can stigmatize people and influence how others treat them. It is important to be aware that this happens. You should know that labeling someone as rich or poor, black or white, or smart or stupid, will actually make them seem even more rich or poor, black or white, or smart or stupid to you, other people, and even to themselves.

This is what you are up against when someone gives you a label. Once you have been called disabled, you are going to be perceived by many others as even more disabled as you actually are. Over time, more and more people will likely treat you differently and soon you might even think of yourself as being more disabled than you actually are as a result of their treatment of you. I am not saying this to depress you; I am saying this to help you overcome it. Knowledge is power. Acknowledging that this phenomenon is at play will help you rise above it, and then you can truly reach your potential even when everyone around you is selling you short, either consciously or subconsciously.

Once you've heard someone referred to by a specific label, it is really hard to erase that label from your memory. Just think about how a jury is sometimes sequestered. Why is this necessary? Because it's a proven fact that if the jurors read something about the case in the newspaper, even though they are told they are not allowed to consider it during deliberations, it has already entered their mind. It's going to influence them even if they try not to let it. It cannot be erased. Labels have this same power. Once you hear them, it is hard to "un-hear" them.

The complexities of the disability label

One of the worst things about being labeled as disabled (or any label, for that matter) is that it takes away your individual identity. Do I have a disability? Yes, that is one part of me, but "disabled" is not who I am; I'm Chris Jones. I'm a person, a son, a husband, and a programmer. I have a disability in the sense that I face some physical obstacles in society. Think about this: are people who wear glasses disabled? I don't think anyone would say that they are. But would they be considered disabled if glasses didn't exist? Then they would be visually impaired, which is considered a disability. The people you know who wear glasses, are they people just like you? Am I?

Why am I so fixated on the disability label? There are approximately 52 million Americans who have a disabling condition and many more throughout the world. This is not something that anyone is dealing with alone, as isolating as it might feel at times.

I always find it disconcerting when a friend or acquaintance asks me, "Why didn't you tell me you had a vision disability." My first answer is always, "You didn't ask me, and we never had a problem where I needed your assistance, so why would I tell you?" It's almost as if they are accusing me of having kept something vital from them. I think this is because they see it as such a defining label, whereas to me it's just one of many characteristics that can be used to describe me. When I run into something that I know is a limitation for me, I ask for help. Otherwise, there is no need to disclose this.

One big issue I have with the disability label is that it is inherently negative. It calls attention to a person's inability or difficulty to do something. It is polarizing in the sense that it immediately puts the person on the "other side" of whomever they are dealing with. Disabled is the opposite of able. And many disabled people are able to do nearly everything a person without a disability can. It is often just one or two tasks or abilities that require more effort on their part.

It is interesting to note that several studies have shown that dyslexic people actually perform some tasks better than people who do not have dyslexia. An MIT study showed that people with dyslexia could read letters written in their peripheral vision better and faster than people without dyslexia. This helps them absorb a scene's "visual gist" much more quickly than other people.

Another interesting experiment involved the artwork of the artist M. C. Escher. Many of his paintings look normal at first glance, but open closer inspection, it often turns out that they depict impossible scenarios, such as water that flows upward and staircases that lead to nowhere. People with dyslexia were able to determine these paintings showed impossible scenarios remarkably quickly; people without dyslexia took one-third longer to reach the same conclusion! This makes the idea of dyslexia as a disability even more incongruous. I don't think many dyslexics feel like they have a gift, but in some cases, it actually is a strength. For example, astrophysicists who are dyslexic can often identify the presence of a black hole faster than their colleagues thanks to their ability to see the "bigger picture" more quickly.

This begs the question: What if disabilities are really capacities that are just waiting to be discovered?

Self-esteem and bullying

I got a letter from someone who read my first book. He told me that he was scared of what other people would think of him because of his vision disability. He's class president and will be graduating at the top of his class. Some people might call him a geek, but he probably doesn't mind much because many girls find intelligence appealing. So what is his worry? It's the image people will associate with him the minute they find out about his disability. Right now he's just considered a "smart" kid, but once they know, he'll be a "disabled smart" kid.

He is doing well in school, and it's natural that some of his peers might already be jealous of him. When they find out about his visual impairment, they might start to grumble. Perhaps he was given extra time to take a test because of his vision problems. He also got the best grade in his class on the test. People will start to say, "He got the best grade because he got extra time." Even people who do not voice this opinion are likely thinking it, because they can't help themselves. First of all, they might not like the idea of a person with a disability outperforming them. People are always comparing themselves to others and making excuses for their shortcomings. It is easier to say you scored lower than him because he had more time than you than it is to admit you scored lower because you were up late the night before watching football instead of studying.

We've all heard stories of young people committing suicide because of bullying, because of the labels placed on them. The bully is really just trying to take some of the victim's self-esteem for himself. He is trying to compensate for some insecurity that most likely came about as a result of labeling. I find it comforting to keep this in mind when someone is bullying me, and I also believe that if the bully felt good about himself, he'd have no need to bully someone else. This goes back to treating everyone kindly and trying to focus on the positive.

The upside of labels

Labels aren't always a bad thing. Sometimes it helps to keep this in mind. For example, it is true that being labeled as learning disabled can lead to low self-esteem, problems with your peers, and low expectations from teachers. However, this same label affords you specialized instruction and extra learning support. Did you know that 15 percent of people are estimated to be dyslexic? Being called dyslexic in a work environment could lead to a bit of embarrassment and judgment from others. At the same time, when a child struggling to keep up in school is diagnosed as being dyslexic, it is often a relief. The child can then realize he isn't stupid or lazy; he just needs to learn in a different way from his peers. Labels can give people hope and even guidance. I am not saying that the good is worth the bad, but it is something to keep in mind when you are feeling down about being labeled.

How can we stop labeling others?

Despite being on the receiving end of getting labeled, I am not immune to occasionally letting a label influence my opinion of someone, at least on a subconscious level. If I hear someone receiving a harsh label, I like to play a little game with myself. I think this is a good exercise for everyone. I make up the person's backstory and try to imagine him as a real person. What is his favorite color? What was his favorite toy when he was a child? What are his hopes and fears? Who does he love?

Remember everyone has dreams just like you. Try to think of the person as an individual first.

I saw an article in the news recently about a photojournalist who made a book of photographs of the childhood bedrooms of soldiers who had been killed in war. I was struck by his comments about how he wanted to show the human side of these people. They are not just more "dead soldiers" to add to the list. Each of them had a story to tell, toys they adored, parents who loved them. We have to treat each other as human beings first and foremost and look past the simple classification to the person inside.

It's also helpful to think about how labels can influence a person's outcome at work: creative, leader, slacker. What about at school with labels like ADD, foster kid, dyslexic? Lots of labels can be ambiguous and are open for interpretation. What comes to mind when you hear the label "cancer survivor" - tragedy or triumph? What about "adopted"? Try to see people from every side.

When you learn someone has a disability, the best thing you can do is try very hard not to look at that person differently and take care not treat him or her differently. For example, if that person is great with math, don't think twice about asking for his or her help with math.

I talk to people everywhere I go and I try to keep an open mind. Say I meet an old person. Old can be negative; a lot of people will think the person is senile or a bad driver. On the other hand, you can view an old person as being wise and insightful and able to share experiences that we can learn from. Once you know that labels exist and how much they influence us, you can use them for good and not bad. Try to give everyone a positive label, and you might soon find that it becomes a self-fulfilling prophecy. This will most likely improve your interactions with people significantly. People rise to meet your expectations of them, whether they are good or bad, so be sure to make them good.

How to overcome labels

When you realize that you are letting other people's labels color your view of yourself, it is a real eye opener. It's like getting glasses for the first time; suddenly everything is clear. Before you got glasses, you might not have even realized you weren't seeing as well as you could. You thought the way you saw things was normal, but now you see that your view of the world was not the best it could be. There was a better version of everything just waiting to be seen by you. The same is true of your view of yourself. Realizing that you can make the choice not to see yourself through others' eyes and putting on the figurative glasses and seeing who you really are is an epiphany.

. . .

It can be difficult at times, but I find it useful to keep in mind that sometimes people don't even realize they are labeling us. I don't want to excuse bad behavior, but some people really can't help it. Perceptions begin to form when we are very young, and as we discussed previously, they are often based on things a person heard in the past, their culture, their experience, or their parents. Lots of things set up perception and there is not much we can do about that. The only thing we can do is acknowledge this is at play and do our best to demonstrate the ways in which their perceptions about us are wrong.

Have you ever thought about what labels other people have for you? What labels come to mind when you think of your best friend? Have you ever asked yourself what labels come to your friends' minds when they think of you, or how they would describe you?

When someone is judging you, it's tempting to think they are a bad person, but it can help lessen the sting of negative comments to try to think about where the person is coming from. Perhaps they are ignorant and don't know any better than to treat you differently. Perhaps they don't understand your illness and they are speaking out of fear. Perhaps they are not evil; they are just confused. Maybe this person is having a bad day. Maybe he got bad news from his doctor. Maybe his dog just died. I find that giving people the benefit of the doubt when they treat me unkindly almost always makes me feel better. You might say I am making excuses for them, but it can really go a long way in helping me to be positive and not become full of bitterness. People can be cruel, but try to remember that everyone has a story.

Another thing you can do to overcome labels is to define yourself. Figure out who you are and focus on your most positive attributes. Try to give yourself a label before others do. You have to resolve to be yourself, the person you really are, rather than the person other people want you to be or think you are. It's a conscious decision that you have to make and stick with. Use the self-fulfilling prophecy of labels and expectations to your advantage!

I'd like to close this chapter with a quote that is often attributed to Johann Wolfgang von Goethe. I think it nicely summarizes what I am trying to convey: *"If I accept you as you are, I will make you worse; however, if I treat you as though you are what you are capable of becoming, I help you become that."*

~Chapter 4~

Education is Key

"Education is the most powerful weapon which you can use to change the world." –Nelson Mandela

Whether you think that the current educational system is good or bad, you cannot deny that there is room for improvement. Although it garners a fair amount of criticism, the system is also doing a lot of things right. However, one thing that I think everyone can agree on is that some positive changes are long overdue.

I feel that education is a topic that deserves a lot of attention, which is why I am going to devote an entire chapter to the subject. You might think, "This doesn't matter to me. I don't have kids who are in school, so how does it affect me?" The truth is that education has an enormous influence on young minds during their formative years. Even if you don't have school-aged kids, today's crops of students are going to grow and eventually become your doctors, your neighbors, your coworkers, and even your presidents. Everyone has a stake in our educational system, and those who think it is not important are being seriously shortsighted.

Consider some of the topics we've already touched upon in this book: success, perceptions, and labels. All of these things are tied very strongly to education. Much like parents, teachers occupy a crucial position in shaping young minds. Educators are authoritative figures that kids look up to, and yet they are humans just like you and I. They are not perfect. They are going to make mistakes; even the most well-meaning teachers might inadvertently steer a kid – or an entire classroom full of kids – wrong. This is why so much attention needs to be paid to what is going on in our schools and how the system can be improved.

Teachers need to embrace change

One of the most harmful mindsets that some teachers can have is their resistance to change. Not all teachers think this way, but enough of them do for it to be a concern. Their thought process goes something like this: "I've been doing it this way for years and I'm not going to change it." Or, "I've been working with disabled kids since the 70s, so I know what I am talking about." I am not going to deny that these teachers have a wealth of experience and do indeed know quite a bit about how to do their profession. That is not in question. I am sure they know much more about it than I do. However, we cannot ignore the fact that education has evolved tremendously. You don't even have to go back to the 70s to see the differences; we know a lot more now and have better tools at our disposal than we did even three or four years ago.

What worked even ten years ago might not be the best approach for the newer generation. Moreover, the laws regarding the rights of disabled students are constantly evolving. Perhaps the biggest change, however, is technology. In the 70s, we did not have computers and handheld magnifiers. Teachers didn't all have the ability to enlarge things on a printer or print papers in different colors, and once these abilities did emerge, they were cost-prohibitive in the beginning. Those are just a few examples, but the number of innovations that are making life for visually impaired students easier is staggering. In addition to the hard work of educating our students, modern teachers must also stay on top of the latest technological innovations that can be beneficial in the classroom. What worked before simply doesn't work now.

In this sense, there are a lot of similarities between my field – programming – and education. As a programmer, I like to take a lot of lower-level approaches to certain issues. Computers and technology change every day, so I make a point of staying on top of the news and understanding the latest technology. This is something I have to do every single day. Not a day has passed that I haven't come across a new innovation that could be relevant to my field. This is a valuable approach for teachers as well, to constantly ask what has changed and how they can incorporate it into their methodology or classroom.

Less dictating, more collaborating

I think one of the best things teachers can do is collaborate. It can be difficult when they spend so much time in their classrooms with their students, but it would go a long way if they could get together more often and share more ideas. Conferences should not involve a few speakers telling everyone what they know; they should entail interaction between teachers and a collaborative environment where everyone is learning from each other. Student-based teaching is one of the best ways to teach and be taught. Everyone can learn from someone else; there will always be someone who knows more about a topic than you do. That doesn't make you any less valuable. Acknowledging that we all have things to learn and actively seeking this information is what helps us all become better - better teachers and better people. It's a give-and-take situation. A teacher's education does not end when they graduate and get their degree; no one's education does. Learning is a lifelong process, and knowledge is power.

American students are falling behind

It's not just disabled students who are suffering; the educational system as a whole has many areas that could use improvements. A number of studies have illustrated how American students lag behind their peers in other countries.

A whopping 29 countries outscored America on a standardized math test administered to 15-year-old students around the world known as the Program for International Assessment (PISA) test. Students from 22 countries scored better than American kids in science, and 19 nationalities outperformed us in reading. I know that America cannot be the best at everything, but these results are bit incongruous considering all of the resources have at our disposal and all of the funding that has been pouring into our educational system. When you consider that Vietnam, a country where 79 percent of students are economically disadvantaged, outscored America in math, it really makes you wonder where we are going wrong.

Perhaps we could follow the example of Germany. After disappointing scores in 2000, a number of educational initiatives were put in place and their performance improved dramatically in 2012. Of course, these results can't explain what we are doing wrong, but they do make it clear that there is plenty of room for improvement.

What can we do to improve?

Experts point to a few things that can be done to make improvements, namely recruiting and retaining top-notch teachers, investing in early education, raising academic standards, and making higher education more affordable.

These same measures would go a long way toward improving the outcomes of students with disabilities. If our schools could attract and keep more excellent special education teachers, spend more money on early education for disabled children as well as the technology needed to help them succeed, and raise the standards they are held to, we could accomplish so much more. We are supposed to be a world superpower, so why are we failing our children?

Classroom instruction is considered to be the single educational factor that has the biggest impact on the performance of not just disabled students, but all students. Given that students with disabilities are facing obstacles in learning and often have gaps in their learning, there is less room for error when it comes to their instruction. In fact, for these students to be on the same level as their peers, they actually need to learn more than their non-disabled peers. It's a big job and it needs to be done right.

One component that can bring about success is being guided by performance standards. Strategies that have been proven by researchers to be effective should be implemented. The students' progress must be continuously monitored to ensure that objectives are being met; if this is not happening, the program needs to be tweaked at once in order to bring about improvements. The instruction needs to be dynamic and exciting to engage students and hold their interest. Finally, flexible groups should be used to tailor instruction to individual needs.

This is something that should be carried across to all classrooms, not just special education ones. More than half of disabled students spend at least 80 percent of their time in regular classes, so every teacher needs to be on board.

Special education teachers have to spend a fair amount of time on paperwork and compliance issues, which is unfortunate because it pulls their attention away from improving their instruction. It's important to find the happy medium in there.

Are some teachers giving up?

One of my own experiences as a child in school stands out. When I was in elementary school, the teacher would come to class and start writing out problems on the chalkboard. She knew I had a vision disability, and yet she chose to seat me in the back of the classroom rather than closer to the chalkboard where I could see well. I would often try to get up to get a closer look or raise my hand to ask the teacher what was written on the board. Every time I did that, she accused me of disrupting the class. It seemed that her goal was to make me act out so that she wouldn't have to deal with me; if I was disruptive, I'd be sent to a different class and she wouldn't have to make an extra effort to help me.

I like to think that most teachers have a genuine desire to help students. After all, no one is forced into the field of teaching. Many people choose to become teachers because they want to enlighten children. But at the same time, I have heard this happening to other disabled students. It appears that some teachers – hopefully a small percentage – find it easier to get the student reassigned by whatever means necessary than to put forth the extra effort required to help them.

Teachers need to nurture a desire to learn and succeed

It's hard not to judge people sometimes, but we always have to remember that we don't know what people are dealing with, as I mentioned in the last chapter. I read a book where a man was on a business trip and a guy sitting near him in the airport had an unruly child. This kid was running around and jumping up on chairs and tables. He seemed like he needed a time out or to be removed from the scene altogether.

The businessman said, "You need to take control of your kid because he's disrupting everyone at the airport." The father of the boy said to him, "I'm sorry, he's having a difficult time because his mother just passed away." This story struck a chord with me because it reminds us how wrong automatic labels can be. The kid was prejudged by the businessman before he had any idea what was causing his behavior. This is particularly important in teaching.

Teachers have a tough job. Not everyone is cut out for trying to keep a classroom of kids under control all day while teaching them things at the same time. But it is one of the most important jobs there is because today's students are everyone's future. The next generation has to be smarter than us. They are the ones who will run the world, who will have to deal with future wars and technological threats. These are the people who we will all have to rely on. We can't lead them to a place where they are completely apathetic. We can't create a generation of students who simply don't care.

A lot of young people seem to think that education is not important. Some of them have reached this conclusion because they sense their parents' attitude that education doesn't matter. The parents are often saying this because they were labeled by their teachers and felt uncared about. This is such a dangerous mindset to pass along, yet teachers have the power to undo it by proving otherwise. To say, "If this student doesn't want to learn, then I'm not going to teach him," fails him tremendously. We have to get to the bottom of why he doesn't want to learn. Perhaps we are not teaching him effectively.

Disabled students are sometimes placed into silos, and this does a lot more harm than good. The Business

Dictionary defines the silo mindset as being a "*mindset present when certain departments or sectors do not wish to share information with others in the same company. This type of mentality will reduce efficiency in the overall operation, reduce morale, and may contribute to the demise of a productive company culture.*" What causes silos? They don't crop up randomly. Rather, they occur as a result of poor leadership. Even good leaders can let them sneak in because they are not aware of what can happen.

Modern education is starting to move away from this trend, however. Shutting students up in a disabled classroom and shutting them off from the rest of the student body does them a huge disservice. It's time to focus on making good silos. I envision this more as different teams made up of people who are good at reading, good at math, and so on. These teams are something that can be built upon because the teams can join other teams to accomplish things. This is an ideal working environment. A team atmosphere might not be the answer to everything, but it is still highly beneficial.

So I was placed into these silos as a kid at school once I reached the age of proper classroom instruction. I was told I had to stay in a particular classroom because of my vision disability, and I wouldn't dare question my teacher. But I seized every opportunity I could to interact with my peers. It took years for me to get out of these silos that other people put me in, and it can still be a struggle at times. It's a defeating feeling, but the only way to break out of it is to never, ever let yourself believe that you actually belong in these silos.

It can be very isolating to be placed into a silo. You feel like no one cares and this is the worst thing that can happen. Once you feel like you can't achieve, others will feel you can't achieve either, and your morale will continue in a downward spiral. Educators have to be very conscious of not creating this and not turning out a generation of kids who feel like no one cares and education isn't important.

. . .

I have a very intelligent friend who dropped out of college. When I asked him what made him quit, he said that he didn't think it was worth spending any more money on college because he wasn't learning anything from his teachers. I know this isn't exactly true; he had learned quite a few things that he couldn't learn simply from life experience, like calculus. A big part of the problem was that he was dealing with a teacher who had the wrong attitude, a teacher who said, "It's my way or the highway". This killed his enthusiasm for learning and broke his spirit.

My friend is not alone, either. Lots of students are dropping out of school not because they are failing, but because the educational system is failing them. According to the American Youth Policy Forum & Center on Education Policy, a third of all students with disabilities eventually drop out of school. A few of the factors cited for this appalling statistic include having to repeat grades, poor academic performance, and insufficient evidence that the school personnel actually care about the students.

I know my friend could have succeeded. I know that everyone can succeed, and I want all of you to succeed – that's why I wrote this book. Don't ever place people into silos. Always think of it as a team approach, because eventually that person will end up on your team, and you want the best on your team. You want someone who is able to learn, achieve, and continue the cycle because life is about continuous improvement. We can't keep doing the same things over and over and expecting better results. We can't let our country trail half the world in education. Teams are the key to ensuring that we become a better society and treat individuals with the respect and dignity they deserve.

Doing things right the first time around

If you did not get the treatment you deserved when you were in school, all hope is not lost. I'm proof of that. You can still manage to succeed even if your educational experience was less than desirable. However, the road is much longer and fraught with more challenges this way. That is why I cannot emphasize enough the importance of a good education, not just for students with disabilities but for everyone.

Labels and attitudes that stick during school years can be very difficult to break free from later in life. Some people never manage to break free from these stifling feelings. I've risen above some unfortunate experiences but I suffered a lot along the way. It is much more difficult to undo these things than to simply avoid them in the first place. Children need to be set on the right path from the very beginning, when their minds are still malleable and their ideas and feelings are still taking shape. It is paramount that our educational system adapt to modern times, that teachers embrace new ideas and technology, and that all students get the attention and assistance that they deserve. The future of all of us is depending on it.

~Chapter 5~

The Role of Society

Our educational system plays a huge role in shaping young minds, but there are a number of other problems with modern society that create these obstacles that we all must struggle to overcome. I want to take a look at society because it plays such a huge role in the way people interact, and this has direct consequences on people's reactions and behavior. Let's take a look at some of the things that are going wrong in society and how we might be able to deal with these issues.

Can't we all just get along?

There are plenty of controversial topics that can be discussed. Religion, politics, and sex are a few divisive issues that come immediately to mind. However, the single most controversial topic in my opinion is race. I don't think that race is an inherently bad thing, but it is something that society has turned into a bad thing for a number of reasons.

When we think about society, a lot of people tend to focus on race. A lot of people have their own opinion about things, but at the end of the day, we all bleed red. We are all humans. Everyone should be treated the same. If only it were so simple!

A lot of people have heard the saying, "Can't we all just get along?" Yet many of them think it's simply a joke. Others are quick to say, "No, we can't all get along because we're different." Well, I would argue that the reason we are different is because we place silos into society as well. In fact, silos are everywhere. They are not just for people with disabilities or people in a certain tax bracket. Society also places people into silos based on meaningless criteria. I've stated before that the key to being a constructive society is working together. A lot of people get hung up on having things their way all the time, and they are quick to cast aside those with differing opinions or those with conflicting ambitions rather than embrace them and work alongside them.

Society is something that changes over time, and individuals need to be conscious of this fact and change along with it. Things that were acceptable 30 years ago are not necessarily going to fly in 2014.

It is pretty clear that society is very connected to the idea of race. Have you ever filled out a census card? There are about 30 different races on there, and these categories are used along with things like education to determine what kind of public funding a town receives. The majority of censuses in the U.S. place a heavy emphasis on the racial aspect. Of course people do have different races and I think it's okay to talk about it, but the problem arises when this is used to discriminate against individuals or groups.

Race and Jury Selection

Discrimination in jury selection is a bit of an open secret. Technically it is illegal to eliminate jurors on the basis of their racial identity, so other excuses are often offered. Although there are some measures in place aimed at preventing this, they are pretty easy for skilled lawyers to skirt.

Prior to a case being tried, lawyers from both sides interview potential jurors to determine if they are suitable. A potential juror can be excused for cause. This most commonly occurs because the juror cannot be objective, often because he or she knows someone involved in the case personally or works in the same industry. A juror can also be passed over using a peremptory challenge, which is when a lawyer can exclude the person from consideration for whatever reason. This is often used to help obtain the desired racial makeup of a particular jury.

Sometimes this happens in a less obvious way. For example, in a capital case, a potential juror can be turned away for being opposed to the death penalty. Minorities are statistically more critical of the death penalty, thus increasing the odds of an all or mostly white jury.

In the eight years leading to 2007, it was found that in Jefferson Parish, Louisiana, black jurors were struck from juries at three times the rate of white jurors. Why is the jury's racial makeup so significant? A study of Florida jury verdicts between 2000 and 2010 found that all-white juries actually convicted black defendants around 16 percent more often than they convicted white defendants. Perhaps even more interestingly, this gap disappears when the jury contains at least one black juror. Diverse juries are less likely to let subconscious stereotypes color their decision, and they are also more likely to challenge each other.

Juries are not the only groups whose thinking is influenced by racial perceptions. In the Netherlands, less serious criminal cases are decided by dedicated "police judges". A study of 365 cases found that Dutch citizens who "looked Dutch" got jail sentences 11 percent of the time, while Dutch citizens who "looked foreign" (including people who were black, Middle Eastern or eastern European) got jail sentences 28 percent of time.

Foreigners who did not speak Dutch got jail sentences more than 50 percent of the time.

It's also important to note how people's preconceived notions play a huge role in their decisions to convict or acquit. It's not just about race. Many of the other labels we have discussed in previous chapters can also influence a person's assessment of one's guilt or innocence. That is why we as a society need to get this right. There is a wealth of data available on the behaviors of juries. A jury is just an example of 12 people, a small group that is easy for us to imagine. Now, imagine when these things are at play in society as a whole.

Of course, race isn't the only way we label people in society. There is also the disability aspect. Like race, a person does not choose to be disabled. Something happened that was outside of that person's control to place them in this group, whether it's a physical disability or a learning disability. Labeling someone as disabled is misleading in the sense that it is something of its own unique structure. People with disabilities are often shunned by society in similar ways to those who are shunned because of the color of their skin. Sometimes it can seem impossible to break free from these social constructs. However, increasing awareness can go a long way toward slowly changing people's minds.

To Help or Not to Help?

One situation that can be complicated for a disabled person is the idea of getting help. Of course, everybody appreciates getting help when they need it. A lot of people will automatically say, "Let me help you with that," when they see a disabled person doing something and that help is not always needed. Although their intentions are good, it is quite likely that the person would not be offering help if you were not disabled. This can be an uncomfortable feeling.

It's human nature to want to help. Some people will argue that there is no such thing as true altruism — helping someone without expecting or getting anything in return, rather than doing it out of obligation or duty. In fact, researchers have shown that when helping someone, the brain's pleasure centers become active, which means you always gain something by helping others. However, the sense of happiness that comes from knowing you helped another person is not always the motivation for doing so. It is often just a consequence. As such, some people do believe in true altruism. Nonetheless, when a person is helping someone else, it really is often out of a sense of duty, loyalty, or even fear of what might happen if they don't.

Regardless of motivation, sometimes people seem to feel a little too obligated to help, and this is what can lead to very negative outcomes. When people try to assist the same silo-ed section they created based on their past experiences, imagine how the people in the silo feel.

When someone immediately offers to help a disabled person, it is often because they feel sorry for that person. This is not a bad thing on their part; empathy is a positive human characteristic that also has ramifications on our survival. At the same time, however, no one likes to feel pitied, and that is exactly what can happen in this situation. Moreover, it's hard not to think that the person is offering help because they are overcompensating for what they feel inside, the burden to themselves.

I have a friend who is in a wheelchair. We hang out often, and one day he told me about something that happened when he went out on his own. He went shopping and to the movies. A friend drove him. When he was trying to get into his car, someone went out of their way to go over to him and say, "Can I help you?". My friend said that he wasn't struggling at all to get into the car. Yet this person rushed over to help him because he had noticed he had a disability. This is a kind-hearted action on the surface, a true example of people taking care of their fellow human beings. I think it's wonderful that someone offered to help him.

My friend declined this person's assistance. Not only was he not struggling, but there was also an older couple next to him who appeared to be in even more need of help. In fact, they too had a wheelchair. No one volunteered to help the older couple, but someone did go to help the younger disabled guy. It's so strange how people are looking for the easier disability to help. It seems that a lot of people are quick to help someone if they think it will require little effort. They can give up a few minutes to help someone and then feel good about them and pat themselves on the back for doing so. It's like they've fulfilled their obligation without really having to go too far out of their way. People want to help, but they are more likely to offer when it seems quick and easy.

The older couple who had a hard time getting into their car was also disabled. They had likely always been disabled and were also growing older, which meant they needed even more help than ever. But helping them would have required a lot more effort than helping my much younger friend.

This tale illustrates exactly what I think is wrong with society right now. I often ask myself, why and how did this come to be? As a computer programmer, I like to solve problems. I want to know what caused something to happen and what can be done to prevent it in the future. That's why questions such as these can be so frustrating to people who think the way I do. It's hard to find clear answers in this scenario, but I do know that helping someone with a disability should be helping someone with a disability, whether they are young, middle-aged, or old. That shouldn't matter. Why does society feel obligated to help one group of people and not the other? An evolutionary psychologist might argue that the younger person has more chances to procreate and prolong the species, so people feel more motivated to help him. But there has got to be more to it than that.

An interesting video has been making the rounds on the Internet that portrays a social experiment. A man in Paris dressed as a homeless man and pretended to collapse on the street to gauge pedestrian reaction. Not one person stopped to help him when he was dressed as a homeless man, even when he cried out for help. When he repeated the same incident dressed as a businessman wearing a suit, lots of people tried to help him. This is yet another example of how the labels we place on people can have dire consequences. People are quick to judge, and in an emergency situation, there is no room for judgment. Some might argue that the bystanders were scared of the homeless man or worried that he was ill or on drugs. These are more assumptions, of course, but if that was their true reason for not stopping, why didn't they at least call the police to help the man?

I've reached the conclusion that this is similar to when teachers place students into silos rather than teams. We do this in society as well. There aren't just silos, but silos within silos. Young, old, women, children. Each group and subgroup is treated differently.

Imagine that you pass two people on crutches. One is a woman and one is a man. Each of them drops one of their crutches. Who do you think will be helped first?

Could it be both? Surely one person can manage to pick up both crutches. However, in most cases the woman is going to be the first one to get the help. This occurs simply because society has labeled females as the weaker sex.

But is that even accurate? Women are becoming heads of households and the breadwinners for their families. They are running their own homes. Single moms are doing the work of both a mom and dad and many of them are doing it well. So why does society still see females as the weaker sex?

I read an interesting statistic recently: one out of every seven men over the age of 18 have been the victim of severe physical violence at the hands of an intimate partner in the U.S. People rightfully make a big deal out of domestic violence against women and the figure for women is much higher at one in four. But it is still extremely surprising that one in seven men have been victims of domestic violence. This is something that men are hesitant to talk about because of the perception that women are the weaker sex, among other things. They often fear they won't be believed or that they will be perceived as less masculine. It is no secret that many women don't report domestic violence out of fear. The number of men who do the same is actually much higher.

A video made by a support group for male victims of domestic violence in the UK recently went viral. In the video, you can see a couple arguing loudly in a public place in London. When the man shouts at the woman and shoves her, passersby waste no time intervening, berating and shaming the man for his behavior. However, when the same argument was repeated with the woman being the aggressor, shouting at the man and shoving him, no one tried to help. In fact, people could be seen smiling and even giggling in the background!

The decision-making process in the male-vs-female crutches situation is fundamentally flawed. Rather than immediately help the person who is perceived as weaker, the person offering the help should have done a quick calculation of who was in more danger of falling. What about the man who dropped the crutch? What are his limitations? Can't you help both? This might never happen to you, of course, but we often find ourselves in similar situations every day. We make these decisions automatically, without even thinking about the forces driving these choices. We learn what has always been done is society, we teach it to others by example, and we show them to treat others the same way and continue creating the same silos.

I recently read about an interesting psychological experiment. Half of the group being studied underwent an eight-week meditation training course while the other half did not. Afterward, individuals were called into the office for an interview, not realizing that they would be the subjects of an experiment in the waiting room. The waiting room had three chairs, two of which were already occupied by other people. The participant would then take the final available chair. Shortly thereafter, a person on crutches would enter the room and make a loud groan of pain while resting against the wall. The other two people were secretly part of the research team and pretended not to notice the person on crutches. Did the person in the third chair give up their seat? The answer is interesting. 16 percent of the people who did not take part in the meditation course gave up their seat. However, half of those who had meditated gave up their seat.

Psychologists theorize that this occurs because meditation promotes the point of view that all beings are interconnected. They feel it is the ability of meditation to break down artificial and divisive social distinctions like the ones I've been talking about - race, religion, and ethnicity and so on - that makes people more compassionate and disposed to help others. As I've said repeatedly, being able to look at other people as equals could be tremendously beneficial to society and this experiment demonstrates that.

Violence in our society

Another big problem facing modern society is violence. Right now we hear about violence in the news every day. There are so many horrific crimes, people shooting up movie theaters, kids shooting up schools. Society is starting to crumble, and I feel this is in large part due to the lack of communication and empathy.

. . .

One big contributor is the portrayal of violence in the media. Study after study has shown that people who are exposed to violence in video games or movies become desensitized to it. One study involved 320 students who were asked to play either a violent or non-violent video game for 20 minutes. Then they were asked to fill in a questionnaire about video games, but this was actually a red herring. What the researchers were really looking for were their reactions to a recording of a fight that they set up using professional actors and played just outside the classroom a few minutes into the questionnaire session. In the recording, two people argue about a romantic partner, and one person injures the other during the fight. The injured person says he cannot get up and asks the aggressor for help, but the aggressor refuses to help and walks away. Once the danger was clearly gone, did the gamers in the study go outside to help the injured person?

It turns out that playing the violent video game did not affect the likelihood of the gamer going to help the person, but those who played the violent game took a remarkable five times longer to go help than those who played the non-violent game. On the surface, 73 seconds versus 16 seconds might not seem like a huge difference, but it could mean the difference between life and death to the injured person.

Another study involved researchers staging an incident outside of a movie theater wherein a woman wearing a cast on her ankle dropped her crutches and obviously struggled to reach them. Everyone did help her, but those who had just seen a violent R-rated movie took 26 percent longer to help than the people who had seen a non-violent PG movie. They also tested out this scenario before the movie and the same number of people helped regardless of which movie they planned to see, ruling out the possibility that the violent movie attracted less helpful people in the first place.

These experiments clearly show that people who are exposed to violent media experience less sensitivity to other people's suffering and take longer to help them as a result. Therefore, one thing we can do as a society to become more sympathetic to others is speak out against needless portrayals of violence. More studies should be carried out to examine their detrimental effects, and the entertainment industry should take note.

The problems our society is facing are very complex. There is no simple solution to all of this. However, it is an urgent problem and something must be done to try to reverse it, even if only in small ways. If things continue on this path, the result could well be even less regard for the wellbeing of others. The effects of this could be devastating to society.

~Chapter 6~

Overcoming Obstacles

When you come across a bump in the road, you have two choices: overcome it or let it defeat you. The key word here is choice. Whether we believe it or not, we have the power to control our feelings. We can choose to be positive and we can choose to be happy. In fact, I feel we *must* make these choices if we want to have any hope of ever succeeding.

My obstacles

As you know, I am an albino and I have a visual impairment. A lot of people are unclear on the actual definition of an albino. People who have albinism have very little pigmentation (or in some cases none at all) in their eyes, skin and hair. This is known as oculocutaneous albinism. For some people, the lack of pigmentation only affects the eyes, and this is known as ocular albinism. The degree of pigmentation an albino has can vary. Some people even note a slight increase in pigmentation in their hair or eyes as they get older, while others might develop pigmented freckles on their skin. Albinos have a complete absence of melanin. Some people are albinoids, and they have just a small amount of melanin.

People who have albinism tend to be quite pale with light eyes and fair hair. The lack of pigment can even make some people's eyes appear red or purple. This occurs when the iris has very little color and the blood vessels inside the eye show through the iris.

Those of us who have albinism are usually as healthy as people who do not have it. Nonetheless, it is not unusual to have vision and skin problems. Abnormal development of the retina and unusual nerve connection patterns between the eye and the brain can cause vision problems in albinos. Many people with albinism have low vision, which is only slightly better vision than being blind. It is also common to experience photosensitivity, which causes discomfort when you are exposed to bright light.

Melanin is responsible for helping protect your skin against the sun's ultraviolet radiation. People who have albinism lack this pigment, which means they tend to burn in the sun much more easily. It is important for people with this condition to take precautions to avoid sun damage. Many of us have to wear hats and other protective clothing and slather on the sunscreen before sun exposure.

Of course, the condition is much more involved than that. I won't go into all of the biological details. I simply wanted to explain the sort of things that I deal with on a daily basis. Everyone has something they have to deal with, and this is the card I was dealt.

As an albino, I look different from other people. This garners a lot of stares when I go out. Some people even take my photo, which can make me feel like a famous person or sometimes even a circus act. As you can imagine, this can take a serious toll on a person's self-esteem. When I was younger, the attention bothered me much more than it does now. As I got older, I figured out that people are just curious and trying to understand. I try to relate that to my own curiosity about things. When I was a kid, I was curious about how electronics worked so I took everything apart and put it back together. Human beings are curious by nature, and this also applies when they see someone who looks different from them.

I'm going to outline a lot of tips for overcoming obstacles in this chapter, and all of them involve taking negativity and turning it into positivity. Sometimes I tell myself people are staring at me because they want to be like me. I always remind myself they are just curious; perhaps they have never seen anyone who looks like me. When I feel this negative energy coming toward me, I try to use it as positive energy instead. For some people, that might entail creating something: a painting, a website, a song. I like to channel it toward my career and use it as inspiration to improve.

Anyone can overcome obstacles

I believe we all have the ability to overcome obstacles. I'm going to start off sharing a story that exemplifies this. It's the story of Rick Hoyt. Rick is a wheelchair-bound guy who was born with cerebral palsy as a result of birth trauma. He can't use his limbs or speak. He was born in 1962, when disabled people were typically sent to live in institutions. His parents bucked the trend, insisting on raising him and taking care of him at home. They faced obstacles at every turn. They had to fight to get the public school to accept him. Engineering students developed a device to help him communicate.

When Rick was 15, he heard about a local college lacrosse player who became paralyzed in an accident. A five-mile race was organized in the student's honor, and Rick decided he wanted to participate. A lot of people balked at the idea of a guy in a wheelchair wanting to be in a race. He says that he wanted to show the paralyzed athlete that life goes on. He enlisted the help of his father to push him along in his wheelchair. They completed the race, coming in second to last. To him, winning wasn't the important part; it was the fact that he participated and completed the race that gave him joy and a feeling of accomplishment that inspired him to participate in other races. As you can imagine, his participation was not embraced by everyone. A number of race and marathon organizers wouldn't allow a person to push another person in a wheelchair during a race. When Rick first applied for the Boston Marathon in 1981, his application was rejected outright. He and his father participated anyway as unofficial entrants. After three years of participating this way, they qualified and were officially allowed to enter. Racing became Rick's passion, and he participated in countless races and even triathlons in the following years with the help of his father. The 2009 Boston Marathon was the duo's 1000th race. They have even participated in Ironman competitions using specially adapted equipment.

Despite his disability, Rick eventually earned a degree in special education from Boston University. In 1992, Rick and his father raced and biked across the U.S. to raise money to help people with disabilities. In addition to the tremendous sense of accomplishment he must feel, he has also helped pave the way for other people with disabilities who want to race.

What does this show us? Rick's story illustrates my favorite ways for overcoming obstacles: changing your attitude, persisting, ignoring the naysayers, and believing in yourself. Rick says that he feels like his disability disappears when he's in a race. I think that pretty much sums it up.

Accepting yourself

Some of the most inspirational people are those who can accept the hand that life has dealt them, no matter how unfair it might seem, and make the most of it. I've learned to accept the fact that this world is not going to adapt to me. Instead, I decided to focus on the things that I can do, even if I have to do them in a different way from most people. As a disabled person, I have discovered that the true disability lies in being insecure and selling yourself short. Accepting yourself for who you are and embracing your abilities is an important step in unleashing your potential.

Actionable advice for overcoming obstacles

A lot of people ask me how I have managed to overcome the obstacles I've faced and accomplished all of the things I've accomplished in my life. There is not one single, simple answer because the truth is that there are several factors that have contributed to my success. I think these same factors can be used by anyone to achieve their own success. When you're facing tough obstacles, a general shift in your mindset can really turn things around and set you on the right path. Here are my top five tips for overcoming obstacles.

Tip 1: Resist the urge to compare yourself to others.

I think comparing yourself to others is part of human nature, and it requires a conscious effort to stop yourself from doing it. Comparing yourself to another person is like comparing apples to oranges. No two people are alike. No two people face the exact same set of circumstances or are given the same set of mental and physical equipment to get through life. That is why comparing yourself to others is always going to be a completely unfair comparison.

Someone pointed out to me that when we compare ourselves to others, we are usually comparing the worst aspects of ourselves with the best things we presume about the other person. The truth is that we don't know that person as well as we know ourselves, and everyone has flaws. Most of the time we really only know what our own flaws are, because other people always try to put their best foot forward. Remember that no one is perfect and everyone has challenges and obstacles to deal with. Moreover, comparing yourself to others is a habit that has no possible conclusion. Even if you are very successful, there will always be someone you perceive as being or having more of something than you do. It's a thought process that you can never win. Comparisons do not add any meaning or value to our lives. Instead, they take away from our happiness, building resentment and bitter feelings.

If you really can't resist the urge to compare, compare yourself to yourself. Yes, you read that correctly. The best you can be is the best possible version of yourself and no one else. Strive to take care of yourself both emotionally and physically. Compare yourself to you last week, last month, last year. Keep trying to be better than you were yesterday. Focus on yourself and forget about everyone else. You can only change yourself. Theodore Roosevelt got it right when he said "Comparison is the thief of joy."

Tip 2: Give yourself challenges and celebrate your accomplishments.

You might not be able to do all of the things that other people can, but you know that there are some things you are capable of. Set reasonable goals for yourself. I like to make a small challenge each day, while also having some bigger overarching challenges to work on in the long term. A daily goal might be something like sending out my resume to a certain company or writing a certain number of words on my website. Big goals can take a long time to achieve, so I like to give myself smaller ones as well. I get a big sense of accomplishment out of achieving them, and that gives me the motivation to keep moving forward with bigger things and boosts my positivity in the process.

When I do accomplish something, I make sure to celebrate. Maybe you're not going to win that marathon, but you should treat yourself if you managed to finish or even just for participating. Choose something appropriate for your abilities and relish in your feats. If necessary, start keeping a list of your accomplishments that you can refer to when you're having a down moment. This can also serve as motivation to help you accomplish even more.

Tip 3: Keep an optimistic attitude.

I know this is easier said than done, but few things have a bigger influence on your outcome than a positive mindset. As the evidence piles up showing the profound effect that being optimistic has on a person's state of mind and emotional wellbeing, an entire field of psychology is now being devoted to positive psychology.

Not only does being optimistic affect your mental health, but studies show it can also improve your physical health! Optimists tend to live longer and get sick less often than pessimists. If all of that isn't a good motivation to try to be optimistic, then I don't know what is.

My friend recently lost his job. It was the third time in two years that he was laid off. I thought he might be depressed about that, so I was pleasantly surprised when he spoke to me about it candidly. He said, "Chris, I can't let this get me down. I can't take it personally. Me getting laid off was a business decision that had nothing to do with me as a person. It's true, I'm sick of starting new jobs only to get laid off again, so I've decided to finally take the plunge and start my own business. I would never have taken this step if I was still at my old job." I was so happy to hear him turn something bad into something good. First of all, he didn't blame himself and second, he used a negative experience to spur him on to something positive.

Optimists view bad things that happen to them as being things that happen outside of themselves. They don't blame themselves. This is a healthy attitude both physically and mentally. And what about pessimists? They see bad things as being their fault and even worse, they expect even more bad things to come afterward. If something good happens, they think they just got lucky and it won't happen again. Think about the optimist and the pessimist. Who would you rather be?

Every day, I ask myself if I'm happy. If the answer is no, I take a look at what is causing my unhappiness and I write down some steps I could take to change this. Then I start putting them into action. When people look at me or laugh at me, I try to keep a smile on my face. It's the best way to deflect any sort of negativity. Just keep smiling, and you can't help but let it all roll off of you. Happiness is the result of deciding to be happy.

Tip 4: Focus on your positives.

Every time you catch yourself thinking of something you can't do, force yourself to name at least one thing you can do to counteract it. You always tip the scales in favor of positivity. Sometimes we have setbacks; we might get turned down for a job or find out we need surgery. When these things happen, think about the upside. Perhaps that job was going to overwork you and make you miserable. Maybe this surgery will reduce your pain or make it easier for you to get around. Turn it into a game. Take every seemingly negative occurrence and try to find the upside of it. Over time, you'll get really good at finding the positives in each situation and it will make you happier overall.

Tip 5: Never give up.

It might sound trite, but persistence really can pay off. Even when it seems like all of the odds are stacked against you, it is important not to give up. As we've already discussed, there will always be people trying to bring you down. All you can do is ignore the naysayers.

There are so many stories out there about how persistence has paid off for people that they could fill an entire book.

Michael Jordan was cut from his high school basketball team. Now he's considered one of the best basketball players of all time. He once said, "I have missed more than 9,000 shots in my career. I have lost almost 300 games. On 26 occasions I have been entrusted to take the game winning shot, and I missed. I have failed over and over and over again in my life. And that is why I succeed."

Albert Einstein was a late talker who struggled in school, prompting concerns that he might be mentally handicapped. He went on to win the Nobel Prize in Physics and his name is now synonymous with "genius".

. . .

Colonel Harland Sanders was a sixth-grade dropout who worked a number of odd jobs before finding himself jobless at age 65. He started from nothing at retirement age to build up one of the world's most successful franchises, Kentucky Fried Chicken.

Many of today's bestselling authors faced numerous rejections. Stephen King's *Carrie* was rejected thirty times. John Grisham's *A Time to kill* was rejected 28 times. J.K. Rowling's *Harry Potter* manuscript was rejected a dozen times. What if any of these people had given up after the first try, the fifth try, or even the tenth try? Rowling told the 2008 graduating class of Harvard, "You might never fail on the scale I did. But it is impossible to live without failing at something, unless you live so cautiously that you might as well not have lived at all—in which case, you fail by default."

All of these people overcame obstacles by persisting. There is no reason why you can't be one of them!

You are the master of your fate

Have you ever heard of the English poet William Ernest Henley? I'm not exactly a poetry-loving kind of guy, but I do find his story compelling. Henley had to have a leg amputated because of tuberculosis, and his other leg was only saved as the result of another painful operation. He had grown up poor, his daughter died at a young age, and he faced a lot of other challenges in life. Yet from this place of great sorrow, he managed to write one of the most inspirational poems of all times, Invictus. We all have our obstacles to overcome, and realizing that we control our outcomes is a pivotal moment in a person's life.

I think Invictus is the perfect way to close my chapter on obstacles. It's short, so please do read through it even if you don't like poetry. Nelson Mandela used to recite it to his fellow inmates. I hope it can inspire you as much as it inspires me.

Out of the night that covers me,

Black as the pit from pole to pole,

I thank whatever gods may be

For my unconquerable soul.

In the fell clutch of circumstance

I have not winced nor cried aloud.

Under the bludgeonings of chance

My head is bloody, but unbowed.

Beyond this place of wrath and tears

Looms but the horror of the shade,

And yet the menace of the years

Finds, and shall find, me unafraid.

It matters not how strait the gate,

How charged with punishments the scroll,

I am the master of my fate,

I am the captain of my soul.

~Chapter 7~

Patience

We've all heard the sayings about patience. Good things come to those who wait. Patience is a virtue. Yes, all of this is true, but it doesn't really tell us how we can get more patience. And the truth is, patience seems to be something that is in short supply these days.

Patience is defined as the ability to accept or deal with delays, annoyances, or difficulties without getting upset. Since most of us encounter at least one of those issues every day, a lack of patience can quickly turn into a major problem that needs to be controlled. It's also normal for us to be on the receiving end of other people's impatient outbursts, which is why a better understanding of impatience is helpful even to the few of those among us who already count patience among their virtues.

To some extent, being patient or not is a personality trait. However, modern society's ability to deliver instant gratification more often than ever is making people expect things to happen faster in all areas of life. When I was young, you could mail a letter to a friend across the country and it might arrive in four or five days. The person waiting for the letter wouldn't panic until at least a week had passed. Now, with the advent of email, everyone wants their answers right away. We've become accustomed to it.

To an extent, it really isn't even our fault. We can get packages overnight now. We don't even have to go to the store to buy a new album when it is released; we can download it from the internet and have every song in our possession in mere minutes. All of us appreciate the way that things can now be done more quickly than they used to be, but we are also all suffering a general lack of patience as a result. I guess you could say we've become a little spoiled. That's why when something doesn't happen as quickly as we'd like, we don't tolerate it well. This is especially true of the younger generation, who has never known a world where letters and packages arrived in days and weeks rather than minutes and hours.

Of course, I'm not only talking about tangible goods. This lack of patience also applies to psychological and emotional things. In fact, these are the types of things that tend to set off our most intense bouts of impatience. When we set a goal, we can't wait to achieve it. We want to lose those ten pounds this week. We want to fall in love and get married by the end of the year. We cannot wait to get that promotion at work. Our summer vacation is eight months away... how will we ever survive until then? There are so many areas in life where a bit of patience is needed, and the truth is that a lot of people just don't know how to cope in these situations.

Disabled people are particularly vulnerable to this issue because they need to be equipped with more patience than the general population. When you have some sort of disability, certain things are going to take longer. You see other people doing things more quickly, and it's easy to get frustrated that you can't do it as fast as they can. The people around you also need to be more patient. Sometimes, a person near you might be tempted to take over and do something for you because they know they can do it faster, and they have to remember to make a really conscious effort to let you do things on your own. This is something that can lead to a lot of tension for people who don't know how to manage patience.

As you probably know, I work for a university IT organization that is outsourced to a third-party company. There is the original group of contracted workers and a few other people who have been brought in to work with us. At one point, I was placed on a project with another worker. Let's call him Peter. At first, he seemed like a nice enough guy who was easy to work with. However, as the project became more and more stressful, he lost his patience pretty quickly. When placed in stressful situations, people start to show their true colors. I want to be clear that I am not faulting Peter for being impatient because all of us are guilty of losing our cool when we are faced with a strict work deadline. However, in some cases, people's uglier sides surface when they are under pressure and this is what happened with Peter. Suddenly he was blurting out comments that were based on labels such as "blind", "stupid", and even "black". I had no idea he was harboring such negative emotions toward me and other people. What used to be a supportive and collaborative environment quickly became a hostile working environment. My opinion of him was forever changed after that incident.

As a person with an vision impairment, some tasks take me a bit longer than some people might like. I even become impatient with myself at times, and I have to actively remind myself not to give up and that anything worth working for will take time and patience. I have taken a few steps to ensure that when I'm in a stressful situation, I can stay on the right path. I try to remember that no one is perfect and that everyone should be treated with respect. This applies to the way I treat others when I am impatient as well as the way others treat me when they lose their patience with me and even extends to the way that I react to their impatience.

As you can see, one person losing their cool tends to have a chain reaction that affects many other people down the line.

Here is a scenario that might be a bit familiar to some of you who have children. You need to leave for school at 8:30. It's been a rough morning. Your son spilled his cereal and you had to change his clothes, clean up the milk, and make him a new breakfast. Your daughter couldn't find her math homework and you had to move all the furniture in her bedroom to look for it. Now it's 8:45. You should have left fifteen minutes ago, and now your son is insisting on putting on his own shoes. The problem is, he's not very good at it yet. You admire his independence but the clock is ticking as he clumsily tries to tie his shoelaces for what must be fifth time while your daughter starts taking everything out of her carefully packed backpack. Finally, you can't take it anymore. "Stop it! Give me those shoes and let me tie them for you! We are late!" you snap. You instantly regret yelling at your kids, and you hate to squelch their budding independence, but you just can't help yourself. You don't know how to keep cool.

This is a particularly familiar scenario at work. You're running late for a meeting and you need that report your coworker has been compiling. You're hovering over his desk, waiting for him to complete it. You can feel yourself becoming more and more enraged as the minutes pass. You're sweating and your muscles are starting to tense up. Finally you explode on your poor coworker, yelling at him to hurry up and admonishing him for making you late. His hands start shaking and he fumbles as he tries to get it done, making himself take even longer in the process. You know it was mean to yell like that and you know you made him feel bad, but you can't help yourself- you're late!

Can you relate to any of these scenarios? The truth is that losing patience not only affects us but also the people around us. Your lack of patience hurt you and it led you to hurt your coworker. It can raise your blood pressure and even affect your health. It can also damage your relationships with others, and in some cases, this damage can be irreparable. It's hard to take back unkind words spoken in anger. If you can see the problem here, congratulations. Admitting there is a problem is often the most difficult step. Now I am going to give you some tips on how to be more patient.

Practice makes perfect

Patience is a skill, and it's something that can be learned. Like most skills, however, it needs to be practiced if you want to see real results. I will give you some real coping strategies when you're having bouts of impatience, but first I want to tell you some ways you can practice this very important skill.

Take a long walk on a quiet trail. If you're always rushing through life, you'd be surprised at how much this will help you. Turn off your ringer on your phone and walk at a slow pace, taking the time to observe and admire the scenery. Focus on all of your senses. Breathe in the air. Smell the flowers. Listen to the birds chirping. Force your body not to rush for a change, and watch how your mind relaxes. It's a good feeling, and it's one you'll want to repeat over and over.

Exercise. Few things can help reduce stress as well as exercise does. I have a few friends who are runners, and all of them tell me that they are addicted to the feeling they get when they run. Exercising makes us feel better. For some people, heading to the punching bag when impatience sets in can help get stress out in a healthy way. For others, walking or going to the gym regularly helps them keep an even temper even when they are not in the middle of exercising. If you feel like you're about to lose your cool, even a quick walk around the block might be enough to take the edge off.

Choose the longest line at the grocery store. Yes, I know this sounds crazy, but it's a great patience-building exercise. Pick the longest line and wait, and you'll see that it isn't the end of the world if you have to wait in line. You might be surprised at how much you enjoy the time you're waiting, observing other shoppers and not rushing into your car to get home.

Skip the drive-through and go inside. If you're stopping for fast food or going to the bank to deposit a check, resist the urge to pull into the drive-through lane. Go inside. Move your body. Interact with people. Americans are known for having a frenzied lifestyle. If you go to Europe, you will be shocked at how long simple banking transactions take. And yet the people there still manage to be happy and productive. Think about it. A few extra minutes at the bank are not going to ruin your life, so why act like they will?

Chew slowly and enjoy your meal. If you're used to wolfing down a burger while you're driving to pick the kids up from school or finishing up a project at work, you are missing out on one of life's finer pleasures. I realize we can't always spend three hours on a five-course meal, but make a point of sitting at the dinner table without any distractions (phone, TV, computer) and actually savor your food. Put your fork down in between bites and focus on what you are eating. Talk to your family. Don't be in such a rush.

Steps to overcoming impatience

1. Pinpoint the triggers that cause you to lose your patience.

What is usually happening when you lose your cool? Is there a certain person or situation that always seems to test your patience? Maybe it's rush hour traffic or your dawdling teenager. Perhaps long waits at the doctor's office or computer problems set you off.

It's normal to blame external factors for your impatience. We tend to think it's not our fault; the co-worker who is taking ages to finish an assignment is the one causing the problem. Once you can acknowledge that the problem is not external but rather internal-your reaction to what is happening around you- you are one step closer to being able to rein in these feelings.

Reframing your thoughts is particularly useful when trying to learn a new skill. We all want to master new skills quickly, but the truth is that most things take time and practice to get right. If you have a disability, the process can be longer than it is for other people, which can be extremely disheartening. Realizing that you can control how you feel about this and you can choose not to let it upset you is a freeing moment. You might even start to enjoy yourself if you put less pressure on yourself to hurry through the process.

Keep a journal

When you find yourself losing patience, try to jot down everything that happened leading up to that moment. What time of day is it? Who are you with? How much sleep did you get last night? Are you hungry? Try to keep track of which situations cause you to lose your patience and then study your notes to look for patterns. Soon you will see which combinations of factors contribute to stressful episodes and you can make a conscious effort to avoid them.

If you're still having trouble uncovering what sets you off, try asking your family members or friends. There is a good chance they have some idea of what things set you off; they might even identify some situations you didn't think of on your own. Your loved ones are often on the receiving end of your bouts of impatience, so they could prove to be an invaluable resource in helping you uncover stressful situations. Chances are, they will be more than happy to help you improve!

2. Look for signs that you are losing your patience.

Here a few telltale signs you or someone else is losing their patience:

- Tense muscles
- Clenched hands
- Short breaths
- Restless feet
- Irritability
- Quick decisions
- Anxiety

When you start to notice yourself slipping, it's time to consult your mental arsenal of coping strategies, which I will outline in the next step. Soon, you'll be so good at identifying when you're losing patience that you might be able to nip it in the bud before these physical signs ever start to show.

3. Overcome bouts of impatience using effective strategies.

When you feel yourself starting to lose your cool, there are a few things you can do. The tried-and-true method of closing your eyes, taking deep breaths, and counting to ten works wonders for some people, but others need to resort to other means of relaxing.

Sometimes simply acting patient is enough for you to become patient. If you start talking slowly and calmly, your state of mind might follow suit. It's also helpful to pause for a few minutes and really think about what you're going to say to someone in that moment. Go over the dialogue in your head before you blurt it out and ask yourself how you'd feel if you were on the receiving end of your words.

It is also important to tell yourself in these moments that reacting angrily is not going to help anything. Traffic won't move faster because you're cursing. The important email you're waiting for from your boss won't arrive any faster because you screamed at your secretary. Being impatient is not going to solve anything, so keep in mind that you are simply wasting your energy. Why not try to save your energy for something more productive, like a good workout later or some games with your family?

When you find yourself losing patience, such as when you're stuck in line behind someone who is chatting to the cashier and taking forever, you need to ask yourself: Is there anything I can do right now to make this go faster without hurting anyone? Usually the answer is no, in which case the next best thing you can do is try to find the upside of the situation. For example, you might be stuck in line but at least the store has the air conditioning on and you're cooling off.

. . .

4. Remind yourself that things take time.

Look at the bigger picture. Ask yourself, will this matter to me tomorrow? Next week? Next month? Next year? This is a good way to put things in perspective. Just how important is the thing you are getting impatient over, and what effect does it really have on you in the long run? A lot of things that we get stressed over are not really that significant. Save your big emotions for the truly pivotal moments and don't sweat the small stuff.

You also have to accept that you're not perfect. No one is. Don't hold yourself to an impossible standard. If you don't get something done on time or don't accomplish something you were hoping to, try not to be too hard on yourself. Everyone has good and bad days.

5. Expect the unexpected.

Sometimes even when you have planned everything carefully and given yourself extra time, something unexpected manages to throw a wrench into your plans. Know upfront that this can happen so you won't be taken by surprise. Try to anticipate any curveballs that might come up. For example, is your layover so short that a slight delay could cause you to miss your connecting flight? Does it take you longer to get to work when it's snowing? Try to leave some room in your plans for surprises, and even then, accept that things could still happen that will throw you off track and that you cannot foresee every possible outcome or control every single thing. You don't have to like it when things delay you; simply tolerating it is enough to move forward without creating additional complications.

6. Enjoy what you have accomplished.

Take a look at how far you've come. By taking stock of all you've accomplished every once in a while, little snags won't seem so devastating when they crop up. Try to remind yourself of all the good things you've done. These don't have to be epic achievements; celebrate even your small victories to help keep that positive momentum going. This sense of accomplishment will help push you through the stressful times and keep things in perspective.

~Chapter 8~

Finding Hope

Feeling hopeless is one of the hardest emotions to deal with because it is difficult to find the motivation to even try if you think there is no hope. Although it is difficult to find hope sometimes, I can tell you that it is not impossible. It doesn't matter what you are facing; you can find hope, and I'll show you a few tricks that can help.

What is hope?

I looked up hope in the Merriam-Webster dictionary, and the definition of the verb was "to desire with expectation of obtainment" or "to expect with confidence". That is a good summary, but I think I like the definition of the noun even better: "the feeling of wanting something to happen and thinking that it could happen; a feeling that something good will happen or be true."

Hope is what spurs us to solve problems and stay resilient in the face of obstacles. It is a belief that we can get what we want or that things can get better. Even the smallest glimmer of hope that our situation could improve is enough to keep us going. That is why it is so important to do everything in your power to cultivate hope.

Even the staunchest pessimist among us can admit that hope is something that can be tremendously helpful to people. Yet it is also easy to lose hope when something bad happens to you. Few things are more painful than dealing with feelings of hopelessness.

Ways we lose hope

How did you lose hope? Perhaps you never had any hope to begin with. I don't mean to say that you have always been hopeless; I mean that you might have always felt hopeless because no one ever showed you how to feel otherwise. Some people do not grow up in a nurturing household and never quite build the confidence needed to succeed. Others start to lose hope after suffering one or more losses, such as the death of a loved one or a financial setback. Some people lose hope simply because they are burned out; they feel defeated and overwhelmed and don't have the strength to cull up some positivity.

One big way a lot people lose hope, especially those with disabilities, is through being belittled, abused, or discriminated against. If it happens often, you might start to think that is how life is supposed to be and you eventually believe you can't control what happens.

Regardless of how you lost hope, I think that dwelling on it too much is not going to serve you well. After all, there is nothing we can do to change the things that happened to us in the past that took away our sense of hope. Instead, we need to focus on the one thing we do have some control over: the future. It doesn't matter what took your hope away- you can still get it back.

My journey to hope

Like many older people, my grandparents are full of wisdom. I still remember my grandmother telling me on many occasions that I should live life to the fullest and not rely on what might come in the future. She stressed the importance of living your life for today, reminding me that tomorrow is never promised to us. This was a good set of beliefs for a young person to be exposed to.

My father-in-law espoused a similar philosophy. He said that we must make sure our house is in order because once it's over, there is no going back. Many people take vision for granted and some people don't realize all that they have until it is gone.

I will never forget the day: December 15, 1977. That was when my mentor and friend Darnell Nickerson told me that I needed to leave school and come with him because he had some important news. That was when I learned that my brother had passed away. It changed my life forever. At the time, I felt pretty hopeless, but in getting through it, I learned that there is always hope. You just have to find it.

I personally feel that hope is something that you want to have and strive for. Since the day I got that news, I started to focus on being hopeful and trying to live my life despite my disability. Although I struggled from time to time, I learned a lesson from each stumbling block and became a little wiser for it.

Unfortunately, sometimes you don't have hope until you've been through a difficult time. This is not the most welcome way to learn, but that is how I received my hope and where I got the drive to go on. Hope is not something we magically obtain. You will not suddenly find it sitting in your lap. The strive to succeed has to come from within.

The bottom line is that you have to believe in yourself. If you don't have this sense of self-belief, you can't really inspire any hope in others.

It took a lot of time and hard battles for me to reach the point where I am currently, and now I want to share my wisdom and knowledge with others and help inspire hope. Once I started to share my life with other people and write self-help books, I saw that I was able to fill a need for people who were experiencing the same struggles I used to deal with. Now that I have figured out how to move forward in life, I want to show others the way.

Do you ever feel like other people are trying to squelch your hope? I find that these people are usually struggling to remain hopeful themselves as they strive for success. It's like a climbing a mountain full of people with everyone trying to get to the top using whatever means necessary. Some people will focus on their own personal journey and concentrate on getting there while ignoring everyone else around them. However, others will push or pull anyone who stands in their way as they scramble to the top. If you've been knocked down, I want to help you get back up again. Many people think that money is a measure of success, but I believe true success lies in helping others reach the top of the mountain.

How to feel more hopeful

I want to tell you a secret about hope. It's something very simple, but a lot of people don't realize it, and understanding it is the key to having hope itself: <u>Hope is something we create.</u> All of us have the ability to have hope. We just have to nurture it. We can't buy hope, and no one can give it to us. Our only choice is to create it within ourselves. Sometimes you might have to look hard to find it, but it's always there for you to see once you make a point of actually looking for it.

In that spirit, here are some tips that will help you generate hope and cultivate it. They are simple things that can have a big effect on your way of thinking, and best of all, they are all steps you can take right now. The sooner you can latch onto hope, the sooner you will start feeling better and be able to take positive steps toward your goals.

1. Take a break from the news.

   Have you ever thought to yourself that the news is depressing? So many horrible things are going on in the world: devastating natural disasters, unspeakable violence, and heartbreaking losses. It can all be too much to hear about, and the constant trickle of information flooding in from 24-hour news channels, the internet, and social media can only make you feel even sadder and more hopeless.

   Why not give yourself a break from the news? If you are worried you'll miss something big, ask a friend or relative to let you know if something monumental is going on that might affect you, then commit yourself to a set period without news of any kind. Perhaps 48 hours is a good starting point. If this sounds too hard, remember: the news will still be there when your break is over. You won't miss anything. But at least try it and see how you feel afterward. If, like many people, you find that the break lifts your spirits, start curbing your exposure to the news. There are few ways you can cut back. For example, just read the top headlines in the morning, and don't read any further into the articles that you know will upset you. I know I need to stay on top of the news for my work, so I seek out industry-specific websites for my news. This can help you avoid unpleasant topics while not falling behind at your job. Be sure to avoid reading the news before bed because you will be more likely to dwell on things as you fall asleep. If you're particularly sensitive to upsetting news, there are even some websites that only post positive news items.

2. Treat yourself well

When you feel like all hope is lost, this is when you need kindness the most. Start by being kind to yourself. Take a long bath. Put on a favorite song or get lost in a good book. Splurge on your favorite coffee or take a walk around the block.

Try to give yourself a little treat every day to help boost your mood- whether it's a few minutes of meditation, a favorite mindless television show, or a phone call to a loved one- and watch how some feelings of hope start to slowly creep back into your heart and soul.

Tell yourself that you deserve to be treated well, and start setting the tone with how you treat yourself. Then cut the people out of your life who don't treat you well, because being mistreated will only lead to more feelings of hopelessness. Treat yourself the way that you'd like others to treat you.

3. Seek inspiration

It's wonderful when something unexpectedly inspires us, but sometimes we have to actually make an effort to seek out inspiration. This is never truer than when you are in the pit of hopelessness and desperation. Sometimes you just need a little spark that ignites the hope that lies dormant inside of you. A lot of successful people will be quick to tell you exactly who or what their inspirations have been. Everyone needs that little push sometimes. Inspirational thoughts and stories can help you realize the potential that all of us have.

Some people find inspiration from their faith. Attending a religious service or reading scripture can help you find hope. Others draw inspiration from the arts. Listening to uplifting music with a positive message can often help us feel better about our own situation, and music has the added benefit of creating a relaxed state of mind. Reading an inspirational book is another good way to find hope. Whether it's a true story about someone who has overcome obstacles or a fictional book with an overlying message of the power of hope, reading something inspirational can help you see a way out of your feelings and sometimes even spur you into action. If there's a particular painting or photograph that inspires you, post it somewhere in your house or your office where you can see it every day and draw inspiration from it.

4. Create optimistic surroundings.

When you are going through a hopeless period, the last thing you need is to have other people dragging you down. If you are surrounded by negativity, this will color your view of the world and cause you to be negative as well. If you are feeling hopeless and associating with negative people, you might need to take some drastic measures, and it could mean temporarily distancing yourself from the people in your life who are pessimistic.

Think of the people you know who are always looking at the bright side of things, people who always have a smile on their face. Try to spend more time around them and soak up their positivity. Optimism and enthusiasm can be contagious, so expose yourself to these people and let some of their positivity rub off on you.

5. Spend time around nature.

   Please don't turn your nose up at this suggestion if you're not the outdoors type. Nature is full of miracles and awe-inspiring achievements. You might not be able to get to the Grand Canyon or Niagara Falls with ease, but there are other ways you can appreciate nature. Go to a local greenhouse or conservatory and admire the blooming flowers. Head to a nearby river or lake and marvel at the beauty of the water. Take a trip to the zoo or aquarium and watch how the animals interact. Spend a few minutes observing a fluttering butterfly or a darting squirrel. It's hard not to realize all the things you are capable of when you see what is possible in nature.

6. Think of all of your accomplishments so far.

   Take a moment to brag about yourself- to yourself! Try to think of at least five things that you have accomplished. Make a list, or if you're feeling particularly ambitious, imagine you are writing a short biography of yourself. Alternatively, you might find it helpful to envision yourself from the point of view of your parents, bragging to friends about all of your accomplishments as parents so often do; what would they say to make you sound good to others?

You've probably never climbed Mt. Everest. I know I haven't. But we all have things to be proud of. Look back at your life. Did you graduate from school? Did you win a basketball game? Do you have children? Did you find courage to walk away from a bad situation? Have you ever won a trophy for something? Did you get hired for a job? Did you stand up for yourself to a bully? Did you help your elderly neighbor carry her groceries inside? Once you start thinking of positive things you've done, you'll be surprised at how quickly more come flooding back into your mind.

When you think of all that you've done, try to also recall the obstacles you faced at the time. Most of your accomplishments probably didn't come to you very easily, and yet somehow you managed to work through the things standing in your way and achieve them anyway. If you could do it then, what is stopping you from doing it now? You still have the ability to succeed; you just need to remind yourself that it is there within you, lying dormant and waiting to be activated by a simple change in your mindset. You might be older now, or less physically capable for some reason, but if you're reading this, your mind is still good, and that's all you need because your mind is the key to finding hope and unlocking your potential.

7. Envision it.

Here's a little mental exercise for you. Imagine that you are on a beach. You're sitting on the soft, white sand admiring the crystal blue waters in front of you. You close your eyes and feel the sun beating down on you, while a gentle breeze tickles your skin and keeps you from getting too hot. You can feel the sand beneath your toes, and you can hear the soft rhythm of the waves and the cheerful chirping of birds overhead.

Were you able to imagine yourself on the beach? If so, then you can see just how powerful our minds really are. The human mind can actually imagine and feel things in the present that we have experienced in the past or might experience in the future. Just like you pictured yourself on the beach, you can picture yourself achieving, and you can picture yourself feeling hopeful. And that is exactly what you should do if you want to be successful and find hope. Having a clear vision of what it is like to be successful can give you a tremendous amount of hope, so try envisioning it and see what happens.

I know I might have made it sound somewhat easy to find hope, and once you set your mind to doing it, it honestly isn't that difficult. If you really want to find hope, you will. It's always there. You just have to truly want it, and it might take some work in the beginning. Just don't give up and keep working through it and you will be richly rewarded with the one thing that can help you move forward and achieve your wildest dreams: hope.

"We must accept finite disappointment, but never lose infinite hope." –Martin Luther King, Jr.

~Chapter 9~

Love and Believing in Yourself

In this chapter, I want to talk about love and believing in you. At first, it might sound like I'm trying to lump together two unrelated themes. Perhaps if you rack your brain, you can see how the two might be connected. However, I am going to show you just how intertwined the ideas of love and self-belief actually is.

It's tempting to simply say that a person who feels loved is more likely to believe in himself, and a person who believes in himself is more prepared to give and receive love. While those things happen to be true, the interaction between love and self-belief is actually much more complex than it appears to be on the surface.

Love makes the world go round

Whether they want to admit it or not, most people seek love at some point (or multiple points) in their lifetime. For many people, getting married or at least finding a long-term partner is one of their big goals in life.

Humans gain so many positive things from being in a loving, romantic relationship. We tend to think of the emotional benefits, but it should also be noted that being in love has positive benefits on your physical health. For example, some studies have found that married couples live longer, possibly because being in a committed relationship can result in less stress and less risky behavior. Physical touch is known to lower stress hormones. Another study showed a reduced risk of heart attack for both men and women who were married. Happily married couples were found to have lower blood pressure than single people in yet another study.

The power of love is also obvious when you consider the downward spiral into deep depression that some people experience when a romantic relationship ends. A bad relationship or loss of love can cause damage that takes a long time to repair. Unfortunately, this is something that most of us will experience at some point.

I think that falling in love is always a fairy tale. It just depends on when it's your turn to fall in love. I suppose there are things we can do to speed the process along, but I also believe that these things happen to us when they are meant to. There are always ups and downs in a relationship, but finding love is always ultimately a magical and exciting thing.

Finding your true love can be a difficult and frustrating feat at times. This is one time where having a good self-esteem can really come in handy. As an albino, it was always hard for me to strike up a conversation with girls. I knew that I had a disability and that I looked different from other people, especially with my yellow hair. This is especially difficult when you're young and lack the confidence that comes with age. As you get older, those feelings start to dwindle, but if I had to do it all over again, I am sure it would still be just as much of a struggle.

A lot of young people don't seem to understand just how important confidence is. In order to have confidence, you need to have hope and faith in yourself. Even though you can't see it, the way you feel about yourself is projected to others. If you don't believe in yourself, other people won't either, and this extends to that girl you are trying to get to know. I am not saying that it is a good idea to act too self-assured, but having a fair amount of confidence naturally draws other people to you, and this includes potential romantic partners.

We can also look at love in another way. People tend to think of romantic love, but there are other definitions of love as well. For example, the type of love you feel for your family members, which are sometimes referred to as brotherly love, comes about as a result of fondness due to familiarity. There is also friendship, which is a form of love that comes from the bond made between people who share a common activity or interest. I think we have to remember to fill our lives with this kind of love, too. Loving others as a whole is so much healthier than not loving anything at all. I know it can be hard to have loving thoughts toward some people, especially those who are not living their lives in a loving manner themselves. However, I think that a lot of the issues we have in the world stem from our lack for love for ourselves or others.

When I see stories in the news about a young man going into a school and shooting his fellow students, I can't help but think that kid was not getting all the love he needed from the people around him. Some people think that people who commit heinous acts are truly evil, and although it's hard to make sense of such incomprehensible actions, it usually comes out later on that a lack of love was a contributing factor. We might find out after the fact that the man who imprisoned young women in his house for decades was abused as a child. The 15-year-old school shooter was viciously bullied. The mass murderer's parents never paid attention to him. Of course, none of this excuses their horrific actions, but it does serve to illustrate how important it is for each human being to feel loved.

The 80/20 Rule: A minority creating a majority

My grandparents were very wise people. They once told me that everything in life follows the 80/20 rule. They said that whenever you try to do something in life, you will always end up with those statistics somehow. Maybe you'll get 80 percent of what you want and 20 percent of what you don't want, or you might be unlucky enough to get only 20 percent of what you want and 80 percent of what you don't want.

It turns out this wasn't just an old wives' tale. The 80/20 rule is a legitimate principle that has been proven using statistical analysis. Thankfully, you don't need to be a mathematician, economist, or programmer to understand it, as my grandparents proved. It's actually pretty simple to understand how it works, and once you can make sense of it, you will begin to see some ways in which you could improve your life.

The 80/20 rule essentially says that 80 percent of your outcomes come from just 20 percent of your efforts. This rule was proven by research by Italian economist Vilfredo Pareto, and some people refer to it as the

Pareto Principle in his honor. Pareto found that 80 percent of the income in the country was received by just 20 percent of the population, and indeed there are many other applications where this simple principle holds true.

Of course, it is important not to get too caught up in the numbers. Even if there was a way to quantify your input and output in exact figures so you can see if it really does break down to be 80/20, doing so wouldn't really accomplish much. The important thing for you to take away from this lesson is the fact that there are certain things in your life that you do (your 20 percent) that lead to the majority of your outputs and happiness (your 80 percent).

When you think about it, you can probably find a lot of examples in your life where a minority creates a majority in this way. You probably spend most of your time hanging out with a small fraction of your total number of friends. Likewise, you probably spend the majority of your money on just a few big expenses like your mortgage or rent and car payment. You probably only talk regularly with just a few of the many contacts you have saved in your phone.

Now that you see how powerful such a small minority can be, you can apply this principle to your life. If you scrutinize your activities, you'll probably find that just a small fraction of the things you do are responsible for the bulk of your gains. Do the four hours you spend each week fishing account for the majority of your happiness and relaxation? Focus on the activities that bring you the best outcomes. Try to avoid spending time on those other 80 percent that are not bringing you as much satisfaction. Find your passions and focus on them, and your happiness will increase accordingly.

This also applies to business and time management in general. Find the most profitable activities and forget about the other 80 percent that are only bringing you minimal rewards for your efforts. Many successful businesspeople employ this principle to increase their earnings and keep time wastage to a minimum. It might mean outsourcing the tasks that are not bringing about rewards so you can devote more time to the most productive things you do in your day.

Since this chapter is about love, let's look at ways to apply this principle to relationships. I have heard people say that in a normal, healthy relationship, you only get around 80 percent of what you want. Perhaps your partner isn't as expressive or athletic as you'd like, but she makes up for it with all of her other positive qualities. You accept this because you realize that no one is perfect. You're getting 80 percent of what you want, so that's pretty good. Some people even go so far as to say that it's the pursuit of that missing 20 percent that leads people to cheat.

This begs the question: why isn't 80 percent enough? Most of us know that nothing in life is absolutely 100 percent. It seems that the people who want that other 20 percent so desperately are often the ones who don't feel good enough in the relationship. This goes back to the importance of self-confidence. They think their partner is the problem, but often the problem is internal. In fact, some would argue that 80 percent of relationship problems come from our own internal issues, while just 20 percent are legitimate relationship issues that arise independent of each person's individual characteristics.

All of this is interesting food for thought. We have to make a conscious effort not to let our own experiences – especially the negative ones we experienced when we were young from our family or society in general – color our view of ourselves to the point that it causes major problems in our relationships. Sometimes we have to change our way of thinking in a big way to let go of the past so we can see the present for what it really is. Sometimes, a problem we think we have with our partner is really about ourselves, and we are the only ones who can fix it.

Low self-esteem can destroy relationships

It's no secret that believing in yourself can give you the confidence to start up a relationship with someone in the first place. Another way that self-esteem can impact relationships is that it can lead to infidelity. Think about it. Most people feel good when they are in a relationship. You can even love another person if you don't love yourself, but you are vulnerable. If you have low self-esteem and someone comes along and starts flirting with you and giving you compliments, you will be so flattered that you might be tempted to test the waters with that person. After all, they are making you feel good about yourself, which is something you might not have been too successful at doing yourself. The fact of the matter is that a lot of people say the reason they cheated on a partner was because they liked the attention the other person was giving them. A person who truly believes in himself or herself does not seek external verification in this way. Some people go in and out of relationships like a revolving door because they are constantly seeking that "high" they get when they first meet a person and feel good about themselves. They don't realize they can also get that same feeling from within, from liking themselves and believing in themselves. They are trying to fix an internal problem with an external solution, and this rarely works out the way they want it to.

Even if you think you can live without love, you still need to work on your self-esteem. Many people, especially those with disabilities, have been on the receiving end of bullying and social isolation over the years. Some of us have dealt with abuse or neglect. All of these things can destroy your self-esteem. People who don't understand the ramifications might blow the issue off, but low self-esteem can impact so many areas of your life. It can not only affect your personal relationships but also your social life and your work life. Low self-esteem makes you more vulnerable to mental health issues such as depression, phobias, anxiety, and eating disorders. That is why it is crucial to recognize when low self-esteem is interfering in your life and preventing you from finding the happiness you deserve.

How to believe in yourself more

Did you know that having negative thoughts is actually human nature? Studies have shown that negative emotions are quicker to form and easier to recall than positive ones, so it's only natural that we are so prone to this way of thinking. Even the most confident people occasionally suffer from negative thinking, but they are able to maintain their overall positivity by recognizing their strengths and focusing on them.

I want you to ask yourself one question: What is your best trait? Think long and hard about what qualities of yours have served you the most in life. For example, your patience might have helped you win over the love of your life and also land your dream job. Your keen observational skills might have made you the hero at work on more than one occasion. Every single one of us has at least one positive attribute that has helped us achieve things in life, whether they are big or small. Figure out what yours is, assess what it's gotten you so far, and then think of how much further it can take you in life.

You will also find it interesting and worthwhile to ask the people closest to you the same question. You might well find that they identify a completely different trait than the one you came up with. Your family and closest friends might see something completely different in you that is also a desirable trait, and by valuing it more, you can boost your belief in yourself. If you want to take this even further, ask your friends and family to cite specific examples of your best traits in action. Concrete evidence can help increase your belief in yourself.

Another way to believe in yourself more is to learn to take a compliment. When someone compliments you for something, don't brush it off and say it was nothing. Let yourself feel good about the fact that someone noticed your achievement and thought enough of it to say something to you about it. If you brush it off, people might stop giving you compliments, and over time, your self-esteem will suffer. Everyone can benefit from positive feedback from others from time to time, so be sure to accept their praise graciously. Tell them that you worked hard on whatever it was and that it means a lot to you that they noticed.

You should also ask yourself if you are determined to fail. When someone gives you advice, do you tear it apart? When a person tries to encourage you to follow your dreams, do you shoot them down with "what ifs"? I have a friend who is dyslexic. He is looking for a job but he doesn't believe in himself. I told him to apply for an opening at a local company I heard about, and he has a million excuses why he shouldn't. "What if they find a mistake in my resume?" "That job is probably too hard for me." "What if they ask me to read something during the interview?" "I always get passed over; applying is a waste of my time." "What if I get the job and I don't get along with my co-workers?"

You see, my friend is determined to fail. His questions and "what ifs" showcase his self-doubts. I want to ask him why he is looking for reasons why he won't succeed instead of actually finding a way to make this happen for him. This job is perfect for him and I think he has a decent shot at it, but I bet you he will never even apply because he simply doesn't believe in himself. Successful people don't play the role of the victim. They believe that somehow, they will find a way to make whatever arises work for them. That inner belief actually improves their chances of having successful outcomes, which in turn only strengthens their self-belief even further. It's a cycle that keeps feeding on itself, and you always come out as a winner when you believe that you can do something. When I first started out in programming, I didn't have anyone to learn from. I was the only person in my family to take this path, and I had to trust that I would figure it all out somehow. It wasn't always easy, but that approach gave me the strength to forge ahead and that's how I got where I am now.

As you can see, surrounding yourself with love and nurturing your belief in yourself can go a very long way toward helping you achieve the things you want in life.

"When you doubt your power, you give power to your doubt." – Honore de Balzac

~Chapter 10~

Help Others, Help Yourself

We've touched upon this before, but it's a topic that is so important that it merits its own chapter. Helping other people and making it easier for them to help you have immeasurable rewards. On the surface, it might seem that receiving help makes your life better, but giving help is actually even more beneficial.

It's human nature to want to help people. I'm lucky to have been on the receiving end of lots of help during my life, and I've also helped balance things out by offering my help when needed. This is part of the circle of life. For example, our parents do everything for us when we are children, and when they get older, we have the chance to pay our parents back by helping them. Giving and getting is an important process and both steps are equally vital.

The benefits of helping

Most of us already know that eating healthy foods and getting plenty of exercise can help us live longer and more fulfilling lives. However, this tried-and-true formula leaves out another crucial component that can extend your life and fill it with more meaning: helping others.

A review of 40 studies that appeared in BMC Public Health found that helping other people on a regular basis can actually reduce the rate of early mortality by 22 percent. That is pretty significant. Moreover, volunteers suffer less depression and feel a greater sense of well-being and satisfaction. Volunteering has the added effect of boosting social interaction, another thing that can have positive effects on your physical and emotional health.

After reading that review, I started thinking about a friend of mine. He has a decent job but he doesn't find it personally fulfilling. He says he feels like he's just going through the motions at work, but he's able to collect a steady paycheck in an economy that is anything but reliable, so he is hesitant to walk away. He recently started volunteering as a mentor to a local teenager, and it has completely transformed his attitude. His job might not do much to boost his sense of worth, but his role as a mentor has brought him a deep sense of personal satisfaction that has carried over into other areas of his life. He's more confident and outgoing than he used to be, which has helped his romantic life, and he feels a lot less negative about his job now.

As you can see, helping isn't just about the person on the receiving end of the help. The helper also benefits. For example, people who volunteer want to help others and make the world a better place, but at the same time, they are often learning something new and feeling better about themselves by taking part.

Volunteering

One way you can reap the personal satisfaction that comes along with helping others is by volunteering. Perhaps you don't know anyone personally who could use a helping hand, but rest assured there are plenty of people out there in need, and many of them don't know you or people like you and that's why they find themselves in need of help. Volunteering can help connect you with people who are in need of what you have to offer, and the beneficial cycle of give-and-take can begin.

It doesn't matter who you are. There is always something you can do to help. You might have a disability - or several - but there is still a way you can contribute. Perhaps you can't lift heavy objects and won't be carrying your elderly neighbor's groceries inside, but maybe you're a math whiz and you can help a local charity with their accounting.

I know that I'm never going to knit blankets for babies in need. My sewing skills leave quite a lot to be desired and my visual disability doesn't help matters. But I'm a programmer, and I can put my skills to use not only for work but also to help others. Nonprofit organizations often need specialized software to carry out their duties, and that's where I can help.

With a bit of creative thinking, I'm sure you can find a way to help others, too. A friend of mine is confined to a wheelchair, but she's a great writer and she writes grant proposals for charities right from her computer at home. A deaf friend of mine is an amazing graphic artist, and he designs the programs for a charity gala that takes place every summer. If you like preparing or serving food, you can pitch in at a soup kitchen. Just think about your talents and the activities you enjoy, and there's a good chance you can find a way to use these skills to help others.

If you want to volunteer and you're not sure where to start, you can usually find opportunities online. However, I suggest asking family and friends first. It's always nice when there's a personal component involved. For example, a friend who runs a pet shelter is always happy when one of us offers to help walk the dogs. You could also ask around at your church. Some businesses partner up with charities, so your workplace might be another good source of potential volunteering leads.

Helping others is especially useful for those of us with disabilities. We are often on the receiving end of help and a lot of us have been made to feel like we are somehow less capable than others. When we help someone, we are seeing firsthand that we can make a valuable contribution to another person's life despite whatever limitations we might have. This helps us to realize that we are capable of doing many great things and can help improve another person's life or just make their day a little more comfortable. This can help alleviate some of the stress and frustration that we encounter in our daily life while also lifting our spirits and boosting our self-esteem.

Another type of help comes in the form of advice and moral support. Those of us who have had struggles in our lives have learned important lessons that other people can also benefit from. A friend once asked me,

"How can I help others when I can't even help myself?" but the truth is that there would be no psychologists or self-help gurus if only people with perfect lives were eligible to help. Even if your personal life is a mess, you might be able to see where a friend or relative is stuck and can help them overcome their hurdles. I've helped quite a few friends work through relationship issues. I've been in a few relationships, some more successful than others, but I'm hardly an expert in such matters. Yet sometimes when talking to someone about their relationship, you'll say something that somehow resonates with them and gives them the perspective they need to handle whatever it is they are dealing with. I love it when this happens. When I'm talking to a friend who is having girlfriend problems and I say something that clicks and he walks away knowing exactly how to proceed or simply feeling better about the situation, I feel an immense sense of achievement. And that is something that any of us can experience. Giving advice to others also helps us explore our own feelings and attitudes. It's a very gratifying way to help other people, and it's something everyone can do. We've all had experiences that others can learn from.

As you can see, there are a lot of ways you can help people, friends and strangers alike. Of course, volunteering too much might have the opposite effect. Help as much as you can, but not to the extent that it infringes on your personal commitments. If putting in ten hours a week at the local youth center is going to make you too stressed out as you juggle work and family commitments, stick to going for a couple hours on the weekend instead. Remember that letting yourself get burned out will do more harm than good.

"The best way to find yourself is to lose yourself in the service of others." –Mahatma Gandhi

Accepting help from others

One thing that a lot of us struggle with, especially those of us with disabilities, is accepting help from other people. The truth is that everyone needs some assistance from time to time; even the most able-bodied individuals in the world can't do everything on their own all the time. For some people, however, admitting they need help can wound their pride. Most of us don't want to be viewed as weak or needy. It's important to push those worries aside and admit when you could use some help. Remember that in asking for help or simply accepting help that is offered unsolicited, you are giving other people an opportunity to feel better about themselves. It might be just the thing they need at that moment in their life. So essentially you're helping them too. Keeps that in mind when you're having trouble asking for help.

If this is something you're struggling with, it is important to examine the reasons you are hesitant to ask for help in the first place. Some people say it makes them feel vulnerable. Others value their independence too much. Some of us are scared of rejection or being perceived as a failure (this goes back to our discussion on perceptions). If you need help with something at work, you might be afraid that asking for it could hurt your chances of getting a promotion or make you appear unprofessional or weak in front of your coworkers.

Perhaps there was a time in the past you needed help and no one helped you, and now you're convinced that people don't help others. Maybe you just don't want to be a burden to your loved ones. There are countless reasons that people are hesitant to ask for help, and there is one thing they all have in common: none of them are good enough!

You need to be brutally honest with yourself and tear apart your excuses. Why do you think asking for help will make you look weak? There is a good chance you grew up watching movies where the hero did everything for himself and overcame the impossible. Even history books are filled with tales of extremely brave people overcoming obstacles and doing everything on their own. Remember that behind every great hero is a team of supporters lending a helping hand, even though they often don't get any credit. The most successful people have help, and they got that help by asking for it. So can you, and who knows what you can accomplish when you are strong enough to admit that you need some assistance?

Another trick that might be helpful when you're afraid to ask for help is to ask yourself honestly if this way of thinking is benefitting you or the people around you. What exactly are you gaining by not asking for help? The truth is that never asking for help can only serve to build up walls around you and isolate yourself from others. You might be perceived as aloof and your personal relationships could suffer. On the other hand, opening yourself up to the give-and-take dynamic with another person can help build relationships and form or deepen friendships. It can help break the ice with someone you don't know well, or add a whole new dimension to a longstanding friendship.

It can also be useful to think about the times you have helped people in the past. Did the other person ask for your help? If so, that should take much of the guilt or weakness out of the equation on your part. But what if they didn't ask for your help? In that case, ask yourself, were you happy to help? Did you feel good about your ability to be there for that person? Why wouldn't you want to give this gift to someone else?

Once you are able to change the way you think about the situation, you are ready to start receiving help. Even if you aren't ready to ask for it outright, you can begin by not turning down help when it is offered to you. Accept other people's offers of help at face value and try not to be suspicious of their motives. When you do eventually need to ask for help, you should choose the person you ask carefully. Opt for someone who is kind and compassionate and not intimidating when you're first finding the courage to start asking for help. Rehearse in your mind what you will say when you ask for help, and then seek the person out and ask them politely. That's really all there is to it, and once you do it, you will likely find it was much easier than you thought it would be.

Help comes in all sorts of ways, some less obvious than others. I am not just talking about asking my neighbor to give me a lift. When I was younger and was first diagnosed as being legally blind, the very helpful Roger Purdy from the Texas Commission for the Blind told me about the many visual aids that were available to make my life easier. Of course, many of these tools have now advanced significantly, but they were pretty revolutionary at their time. From talking calculators to magnifying tools and bioptics, there were so many things available that could help me cope with daily life and I was eager to take full advantage of them. I know I could have never accomplished what I have in my life without that help. This is how I can say with great confidence that people who shun help are only hurting themselves. I also know that even with this help, my accomplishments are still my own because I provided the hard work, motivation, and persistence needed to reach my goals.

Believe me, I know how annoying it can be when a well-meaning friend or family member wants to take over and do everything for you. There are plenty of things I can do for myself, and it is indeed a little frustrating when someone wants to do everything for me. In those moments, I just try to remind myself that their offer to help is not necessarily an implication that I can't do anything. It's often just a matter of the person offering the help wanting to feel useful. I have found that accepting help even when I don't need it actually benefits everyone involved.

Turning down help gracefully

Of course, even with what I said above in mind, there will still be some times when you simply do not want help. Perhaps someone wants to help you in the bathroom or wants to take over a task you had actually been looking forward to doing yourself. There are a few ways to politely reject their offer without hurting their feelings or harming your chances of getting help from them in the future.

Begin by acknowledging the good intentions behind their offer. You could start by saying something like, "It's very kind of you to want to help me with that, but this is something I really need to do myself." Perhaps you can think of something else the person can do so they can still feel useful. "While I'm taking care of this, would you mind taking the dog outside for a few minutes?" This allows you to keep control over the task at hand while still letting the other person feel needed, and can also earn you a little bit of alone time, which can be useful when overbearing relatives are around.

If for some reason you can't or don't want to redirect them to another task, gently turn down their offer while leaving the door open for future help. "Thanks so much for offering to drive me to the store, but I've got this under control. I have a business trip next week; perhaps you can give me a ride to the airport then?" Or "It's very generous of you to offer to take out my garbage but I could really use a few minutes of fresh air anyway. I'll let you know the next time I need something."

Sometimes people offer to help because they genuinely don't know what you're capable of. I had a friend who was always offering to give me rides places. I appreciated the sentiment, but I can drive and I don't like depending on other people for things I can do myself. Finally, I told him I can drive with the help of bioptic lenses. He had actually never heard of such a thing, and when I showed them to him, he thought they were pretty cool. I'm so glad I didn't simply get frustrated and curtly tell him I don't need help. My polite rejection of his help actually turned into a "teachable moment" and we were able to bond while cracking jokes about the aesthetic qualities of my bioptics. After that, he stopped offering to give me rides, and I even drove him home once!

Helping change perceptions

Let's return to the idea of preconceived notions. We already know that it's not easy to change people's perceptions of us. But there are things we can do to make that job easier and there are also things we might be doing – perhaps unwittingly – that only serve to reinforce their ideas. When faced with someone who has misjudged you, a cool head and a lot of patience can help both of you. By showing that person your true self, you are helping them realize the error of their judgment and possibly preventing them from making the same mistake again. At the same time, you are helping improve their perception of you by showing them who you really are rather than reacting negatively and hurting your image in their eyes. It's a win-win situation!

As you can see, learning to give and get help are some of the most valuable and worthwhile lessons you will ever learn.

"No one is useless in this world that lightens the burdens of another." –Charles Dickens

~Chapter 11~

Looking Forward

I think that looking forward is an appropriate theme for the last chapter of my book. After all, focusing on the past can only get us so far. It's useful to know how we became the way we are and understand the role that our early influences played in shaping us, but nothing is more important than looking to the future. This is because we cannot do anything to change the past. The things that have happened to us cannot be undone. However, there is so much we can do to change the future, and we can start building that future today if we manage to let go of things from our past that are holding us back. Even if you have a disability, you still have every ability to create a good outcome for yourself. How empowering is that?

Mind over matter

I know how hard it can be to resist the temptation to dwell on the past. We've all struggled and we've all faced hard times. It's easy to get caught up in thinking about particularly traumatic things that have happened to us. When I find these negative thoughts entering my mind, I try to recognize them for what they are. If I am dealing with a particularly intrusive thought or memory that I know I am prone to dwell upon, I will sometimes even go so far as to set a timer. I know that might sound extreme, but dwelling on the past doesn't solve anything. If I can't seem to get the thought out of my head, I will set a timer on my cell phone for five minutes. During those five minutes, I let myself go back in time. I go into the darkest corners of my mind and dredge up those nagging thoughts and confront them head on.

When the buzzer sounds to indicate that the time is up, do you know what I do? I set it for another five minutes. I make myself use the next five minutes just as intensely to focus on what I can do to make my future better. I'll dream, plan, and try to think of at least one thing I can do by the end of the day to take a step toward my goal, no matter how small that step might be. Perhaps I can't run a marathon or write a chapter in my book before sundown, but I can find the time to send an email about a job opening or call an old colleague to propose a project. In doing this, I am balancing out thinking about the past with thoughts of the future. Of course, eventually you want to shift your mindset so that you spend a lot more time thinking about the future than the past. Eventually you might decide to let yourself think about the past for three minutes and the future for seven minutes. Over time, you might even find it easy to push those destructive past thoughts of your mind completely and lose yourself in thoughts of the future. That's when you'll know you have truly mastered the ability of putting mind over matter.

Familiarity breeds comfort

Life is constantly changing and evolving, morphing into something new and adventurous. Sometimes it might feel like it's hard to stay on top of everything and you need to stop and catch your breath. It can be difficult to take that leap of faith and move forward to the next big thing in life. This is something that I have always struggled with. Like many people, I feel a sense of comfort in things that are familiar, and it is easy to fall into the trap of convincing myself that where I am and what I am doing is safe.

In fact, this phenomenon is so prevalent that it has been labeled and studied in depth by psychologists. It's called the mere exposure effect, and it states that familiarity not only creates comfort but also reassurance and even relief. After we are repeatedly exposed to something – even if it is something bad – we eventually become comforted by it, whether it is an object or a person. This is how so many people end up staying in a job they hate or unable to break free from a bad relationship. Even if we are in a bad situation, we know what we have to deal with right now; we don't know what we'll end up with if we make a change. This fear of the unknown keeps us in these negative situations without us even realizing it sometimes.

The mere exposure effect has a lot of interesting implications. For example, the more often we see a person, the more likeable and pleasing they appear to us. It's also useful to advertisers who want us to buy their products simply because we've heard their name before. Investors often opt to place their money on domestic companies because they are familiar with them rather than looking into unknown international companies that might offer better returns. Have you ever heard a publicist saying, "There is no such thing as bad publicity"? All of these are examples of how we are comforted by things that are familiar to us, so you are definitely not alone if you are resisting making a change because you feel safe with the status quo in your life.

You can use your knowledge of the mere exposure effect to our benefit. Rather than latching on to familiar things are not good for us, we can seek out comfort from more constructive endeavors. Maybe it's going fishing to remind you of fun times you had with your grandfather as a child, or hanging a favorite painting in your living room that reminds you of a happy time in your life. These acts, although they seem so small, can actually go a long way toward giving us the sense of inner peace we need to chase our dreams or even just get through a bad day.

I know I have used my vision disability to help me move forward in life. If something is new and scary to me because I have never done it before or I don't have enough vision to do it, this always pushes me to do it even more now that I know the things I have learned about life. Yes, trying new things is almost always difficult to some degree, but I also know that wisdom comes from experience and I think wisdom is a very desirable trait. I also find it helpful to keep in mind that if it was easy, everyone would do it.

I hope that one of the most important things you will take away from my book is being able to always look for the next thing you can accomplish. I was told throughout my life that I would never succeed. This was ingrained in me from an early age, and for the longest time, I truly believed it. Eventually I learned that it was not my disability that was holding me back but it was actually my mindset! Everything keeping me from success was in my head, and I had the power in me to change my thoughts all along. Once I did that, I started getting the results I wanted. Sometimes a person gets programmed to believe that they are incapable by people in positions of influence and power in their life, and as a result, they have trouble moving forward. I know that everyone can be successful as long as they make sure they are measuring their success appropriately.

Tying it all together

As I've gotten older, I've realized that is not money, fame, or women that make a person successful, as I touched upon in previous chapters. Being happy or successful actually lies within you as a person. I always thought that being rich or famous or having my book on the *New York Times* best-seller list would be a dream comes true, but after I released my first book, *The*

Insight of Perseverance, I had a major insight of my own. I realized that I touched the lives of most people who read it. I gave them the hope to believe that they could succeed in life and believe in their ability to reach their goals. This ended up being even more satisfying to me than any financial rewards I might have obtained from the book, and I'm hoping to repeat that success with this one by enlightening and inspiring my readers. I love to hear personal stories of victory and accomplishment from my readers. Nothing makes me feel better than knowing that I helped someone else chase their dream.

I would love to be able to tell you that once you realize what makes you happy, success will come easily. Unfortunately, that's not really the case. Figuring out what makes you happy is always a worthwhile endeavor, but it's not enough on its own. There is a lot of work to be done if you want to achieve success and those who start moving forward rather than sitting around and feeling intimidated by the amount of work involved are the ones who will reach the top.

Remember that a journey of a thousand miles begins with a single step. Don't let yourself get left behind or lost in the shuffle; create a realistic plan and start putting it into action today. Don't expect instant gratification. It can happen overnight for some people, but that is the exception, not the rule. Accept that you will struggle, but these hurdles will only make you stronger.

I hope that I have given you the tools you need to achieve your wildest dreams- and beyond. Now that you know the effect that perceptions and labels have on you, you can move past them and keep your eyes on the prize. Don't let the opinions of others define you. We can take the things that people say with a grain of salt and shrug off hurtful comments now that we know where these people are coming from. When someone says something hurtful to you, I hope you will turn to that chapter of my book, read it again, and remind yourself exactly why you shouldn't let it get the best of you.

We've also examined how society and our educational system can shape people. When we are dealing with schools, teachers, or other people in general, we can now do so with our eyes open. Others might try to place us in silos, especially those who are coming from a place of ignorance, but we know that we can push beyond these boundaries and fulfill our untapped potential even when it feels like the rest of the world is aligning against us. People can't keep us down unless we let them. That has been a tough lesson for me to learn, but it's also one of the most valuable ones.

I hope that after reading my chapter on patience, you will have a better appreciation for the fact that good things come to people who wait. We can be more patient with others and, more importantly, ourselves as we make our way through this journey using the tricks that I outlined for keeping your cool, and our relationships with ourselves and others will improve as a result.

I also wanted to instill each and every one of you, my readers, with hope, because without it, there is little chance of ever becoming what you want to be. The final piece of the puzzle, of course, is loving yourself and others and believing in yourself. I think all of these factors give you the foundation you need to become what you were always meant to be.

I want to leave you with a quote from Helen Keller, who achieved so much in her life despite being blind and deaf. She might not have been able to see, but she had incredible insight. She said, "Character cannot be developed in ease and quiet. Only through experience of trial and suffering can the soul be strengthened, ambition inspired, and success achieved."

ABOUT THE AUTHOR

Christopher Thomas Dwight Major Jones is the son of Major and Sherry Jones. He attended school in Winona, Texas, a little town near Tyler, Texas where he was born on December 18, 1983. In 2002, Christopher graduated high school in Winona, Texas and continued his education at the Texas State Technical College in Marshall, Texas. After 6 years at the college, Christopher received his associate's degree in Software Engineering.

Then in 2008, after successfully completing his studies in Computer Information Systems at Texas A&M University in Commerce, Texas, Christopher received his Bachelor's degree. Following his undergraduate studies, he worked in the field of Computer Science as an Application Web Developer, which led to his enrollment into the Master's program in Computer Science there at Texas A&M University.

Shortly after graduation in 2010 with his Master Degree in hand and still at Texas A&M, Christopher began exploring his computer background. He combined his hardware and software experiences which led to his research and development of new ideas. Christopher started to prototype a device that would store energy and also help the environment by harvesting the energy using a microcontroller. He developed a sensor node capable of running any type of code while maintaining its efficiency in energy harvesting. In 2010, Christopher applied for a patent on ideas and concept of a new efficient way to store power in a rechargeable environment. The patent is currently pending in the United States Patent Office while Christopher is currently working on his PHD and teaching at Texas A&M University. Chris is also the founder of the Bling Tec Foundation helping companies and moving the cause forward for assistive technology for students with disabilities.

Visit My Website:

http://perception.joneschris.info/

Follow Me on Twitter: Defjam903

Like Me on Facebook

https://www.facebook.com/joneschris903

. . .

Ideals are like stars. You will not succeed in touching
them with your hands, but, like the seafaring man,
you choose them as your guides, and, following them,
you will reach your destiny.

R.I.P Henry Lee Marshall

Everybody really knows what to do to have his life filled with joy. What is it? Quit hating people; start loving them. Quit being mad at people; start liking them. Quit doing wrong; quit being filled with fear. Quit thinking about yourself and go out and do something for other people. Everybody knows what you have to do to be happy. But the wisdom of the test lies in the final words: If ye know these things, happy are ye if ye do them. – Rev. Norman Vincent Peale

Perception Notes.

After reading this book uses this section to help you have a better perception about life each other and yourself.

_____

_____

_____

_____

_____

_____

_____

_____

_____

_____

_____

_____

_____

_____

_____

www.ingramcontent.com/pod-product-compliance
Lightning Source LLC
Chambersburg PA
CBHW051827090426
42736CB00011B/1689